All Stressed Up and Everywhere to Go!

Solutions To De-Stressing Your Life and Recovering Your Sanity

Gaylyn R. Williams
Ken Williams, Ph.D.

Relationship resources

empowering people for maximum success in all their relationships

Contact Relationship Resources for additional copies and quantity discounts:
  PO Box 63383
  Colorado Springs, CO 80962
  www.RelationshipResources.org
  Stressbook@RelationshipResources.org

Cover designed by Nathan Fisher. www.NathanFisher.net

ISBN 9780972172875

Printed in the United States of America.

I recommend you take the time to read this important book. Stress can ruin your life, but Jesus offers a better way The Biblical solutions and personal truths in this book can set your heart, mind and soul free. This book is a timely remedy for a culture consumed with pressure, over-scheduling, impossible deadlines and sleepless nights full of anxiety. Read and be restored to the life God intended.

—*Gary Wilkerson*, President of World Challenge
and Pastor of The Springs Church

Dr. Ken Williams is an expert in dealing with issues related to stress and its impact on our lives. He draws from a deep well as he writes having spent years as a Wycliffe missionary himself, and then as a counselor to missionaries. He combines his life experience, professional training, and academic credentials to co-author a book full of solid advice. He and daughter, Gaylyn, have teamed up to provide an excellent resource for believers who want to de-stress their lives through the application of God's Word mixed with healthy counseling principles.

—*Bob Creson*, President and CEO,
Wycliffe Bible Translators USA

Serving as a pastor for nearly thirty years, I am always on the lookout for those resources that are solidly rooted in Scripture and intensely practical for myself and for those to whom I minister. Because the principles flow out of God's Word, they are timeless and relevant in any context. And thanks to the authors' special knack for clear communication, the principles are easy to grasp and easy to hand off to others who are in the "stress crucible."

—*Tim Westcott*, Pastor of Idyllwild Bible Church

This father/daughter writing team have produced something profoundly useful for the Christian community. It will bless and help anyone who studies it. Ken is a legend in Wycliffe Bible Translators. My husband and I have known him for 40 years. He lives the principles expressed in this book. So does Gaylyn. The diversity of their experience strengthens the book and enhances its usefulness. Authentic, soundly practical, occasionally funny, often heart-wrenching—you'll love it!

—*Laura Mae Gardner*, D.Min., International Training
Consultant for Wycliffe Bible Translators and SIL International

This excellent, distinctive book is grounded in Scripture, rich with examples and clearly born from the crucible of experience. The blending of principle, insight and encouragement makes it readily understandable and invitingly applicable. It is at the same time both text and workbook, promising to be helpful to anyone seriously wishing to better handle stress for themselves and/or assisting others in the too common experience of being "all stressed up". A thoughtful and timely contribution to understanding stress and doing something about it!

—John Powell, Ph.D. Psychological Consultant to Missions,
Professor Emeritus, Michigan State University,
Co-Founder, Annual Conference on Mental Health and Missions

I was so captured by this material that our church hosted a week long workshop in which 27 of our lay caregivers and 4 vocational staff members received training in this material. We all found it extremely helpful in equipping us in our ministry to others and it has been passed along to many others. More than 11 years later I still find the material beneficial in my personal ministry and as I equip others to minister. The material is as relevant and helpful today as it was then. Most importantly it equips one to develop strategies and skills for managing stress in a life giving manner.

—Wayne Cone, Pastor of Pastoral Care, Cypress Bible Church

As a counselor, I am always looking for topic specific books that deliver helpful insights with practical application. *All Stressed Up* is the most comprehensive, functional stress management book in my lending library. I've got a bunch on the subject but this one is my first choice for homework assignments.

—Tim Sieges, Phd., Counselor with Wycliffe Bible Translators

All Stressed Up and Everywhere to Go is written in such a personal manner that you will feel as though you are sitting with Ken and Gaylyn and being encouraged to fully understand, apply and share the principles clearly outlined. As a veteran of over 30 years including a tour flying combat helicopter missions in Viet Nam, serving in several foreign lands, with and separated from my beloved family and frequently faced with the pressures of decision making then and in executive positions since, I wish this extraordinary book had been available to me.

—John Coats, Colonel U.S. Army (Ret)

Dedicated to all our missionary friends worldwide,
in stressful situations, who are successfully applying these
biblical principles.

Let us fix our eyes on Jesus,
the author and perfecter of our faith,
who for the joy set before him
endured the cross, scorning its shame,
and sat down at the right hand
of the throne of God.
Consider him who endured
such opposition from sinful men,
so that you will not grow weary and lose heart.
Hebrews 12:2-3

Table Of Contents

Part Four: Recover Your Sanity

Foreword by Jerry Bridges

Stress is a fact of life. The question is not whether we will experience stress—that is inevitable. The question is how we will respond to it. Most of us do not handle stress well because we do not know how. But now, relief is at hand. This book, if studied and applied, will provide you with the principles you need to manage your stress effectively.

This book is valuable for at least three reasons.

First, it is thoroughly biblical. All its teaching is based squarely on biblical text and principles. I have known Ken Williams for well over 50 years, and I know that he has always been a careful and thoughtful student of the Scriptures. God, who created human beings in the first place, understands us completely. He is, so to speak, the infinitely wise Master Psychologist. He has provided in His Word the principles we need for handling stress.

Second, this book is practical. It speaks to real-life situations and provides real-life solutions. It takes you by the hand and leads you step by step in identifying your causes of stress and provides strategies for dealing with them.

> **This book is valuable for at least three reasons. It is thoroughly biblical, practical, and authentic.**

Third, this book is authentic. Both Ken Williams and his daughter Gaylyn have experienced an extraordinary amount of stress in their respective lives. They do not write from the vantage point of academic theory—although Ken, with a Ph.D. in human behavior, could do that—but from the reality of applying these biblical principles to the stressful situations of their own lives.

I must add one word of caution, though. If all you plan to do is read this book, don't bother. This book is designed as a *workbook*, not just a book to be read and set aside. To benefit from it, you must work at identifying the stress issues in your life and applying the principles in this book for dealing with them.

As I looked through the manuscript in preparation for writing this foreword, I identified two significant stress points in my life. I now have a plan for dealing with them. I hope this book will have the same effect on you.

Jerry Bridges
Staff Development, The Navigators
Author of over 15 books, including *The Pursuit of Holiness*,
which has sold over one million copies

Introduction

Bright lights suddenly bore down on me (Gaylyn), blinding me. I had just started turning left with the green arrow in my 1967 Dodge Dart. *What should I do? Step on the gas? There's no way I'll get out of the way. He's coming too fast.*

My body tensed with fear. I cried out, "God, I need your help. I don't wanna die."

BLAM! My car spun around, ending up 50 feet behind the crash. Instantly it was deathly quiet. The impact stunned me as my knee flattened the key in the ignition and my head compressed the steering wheel. I struggled to keep consciousness. *I can't die. I just can't die. I'm going to be a missionary. God help me.*

"Ouch!" I ached all over. Feeling blood dripping off my chin, I reached up and touched new holes in my face. *Oh no, not my face. I'm getting married in a month.*

I was almost home from college for the weekend. My week had been stressful as I was finishing everything before graduation in less than a month. Between school work and finishing my thesis,

I was also finalizing the details for my wedding—a week after graduation.

People began running toward my car as I tried to open the door. *Groan. I hurt all over.*

As if in a tunnel, words echoed in my brain, "I can't believe she is alive. No one should have lived through that."

The sirens screamed in the distance, coming closer. "Someone must have been looking out for you," a short, plump woman said, as she opened my door.

As the police arrived, the tall, dark man who hit me got out of his car, unhurt. I stared in amazement as he started running up the embankment. The officers raced after him, tackling him to the ground. Walking back to their patrol car with the disheveled man, one said, "Whoa! The alcohol on his breath could almost knock me out."

I finally managed to get myself out, but had to grab the car door to keep from fainting. The ambulance, with its bright, flashing lights and wailing siren, stopped a few feet from me. The kind-faced paramedic put his arm around me, holding me upright as we walked to the ambulance. After quickly checking me, he said, "We've got to get her to the emergency room."

"No! Just call my parents. They'll take me. I don't want my parents to have a huge ambulance bill."

"You've got to be kidding," someone behind me said.

After they called my parents, I asked, "Can you please clean as much blood off me as you can? I don't want my mom freaked out."

Stress is a major problem, affecting people more each year.

"We'll do our best, but it won't be perfect."

When my parents arrived at the accident scene, I saw tears in my mom's eyes. At the hospital, the admitting doctor checked me. He announced, "I'll sew her face up and then she can go to a plastic surgeon later." Amazingly, nothing was broken.

"But she's getting married in a month!" My mom insisted they call a plastic surgeon immediately to put my face back together.

Over the next few weeks, my body healed, despite massive bruising and pain that became arthritis a few months later. *Thank you, Lord, for my seatbelt, and the interesting bruises it caused!* To this day, I'm thankful for the faint scars on my face, reminding me of God's grace, faithfulness and protection.

Just like my car wreck, things happen that are out of our control, causing us trauma and anxiety. Stress is a major problem, affecting people more each year. The American Psychological Association recently found:

- 75 percent of adults experienced moderate to high levels of stress in the past month.

- 42 percent said their stress had increased in the past year.[*]

As you'll discover, stress itself is not bad. How you react to it is what affects you. There are many ways to respond to stress, some more beneficial than others. One way to react is by taking the advice of an old Navy slogan: "When in danger or in doubt, run in circles, scream and shout." I don't know about you, but I've never found that method works too well.

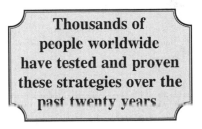

Thousands of people worldwide have tested and proven these strategies over the past twenty years

Have you ever felt like you were *all stressed up with everywhere to go*? You have too much to do and don't even know where to start. Does stress run your life? Are you ever paralyzed with feelings of being overwhelmed? Maybe you even begin to run in circles, scream and shout. This book gives practical strategies to keep from getting all stressed up so you can have a more successful and joy-filled life.

Although many volumes have been written about stress, thousands of people worldwide have tested and proven these strategies over the past twenty years. Besides teaching workshops on these principles, nationally and internationally, we both regularly apply them to our personal lives.

While there are many great secular principles for managing stress, the Bible lays the foundation of this practical book. We encourage you to study what the Word says, because it is the best manual on managing stress. As Hebrews 4:12 says, "The Word of God is living and active." It has the power to equip you to handle all your stress.

Each person brings expectations and assumptions to this study. This book won't meet every expectation, and every assumption won't turn out to be accurate. We encourage you to hold your expectations in an open hand to the Lord. Let Him do whatever He wants in your life during your study. God undoubtedly has expectations and plans for you that you don't yet know about, but we can trust Him to reveal and bring them to reality.

Our desire is to give you the practical, biblical tools you need to effectively manage stress, so you can be more successful in every area of your life. We are praying the Lord will use these pages to bless and empower you as you follow Him.

Ken L. Williams, Ph.D.
Gaylyn R. Williams
A father-daughter writing team

Note: For simplicity, masculine forms are used to designate both genders in some chapters.

* Copyright ©2009 by the American Psychological Association. Stress in America 2009. Washington DC. Adapted with permission. Apa.org/news/press/releases/stress-exec-summary.pdf. No further reproduction or distribution is permitted without written permission from the American Psychological Association.

How to Use This Book

This is an interactive workbook. If you want to reduce your stress levels, you need to dedicate the time needed to study each section and do the assignments given.

Each chapter ends with a personal application section called, "What can I do today?" We want to encourage you to apply what you are learning, so that you can de-stress your life.

Every chapter also has a section called, "Questions for personal or group study." If you are studying in a group or with one other person, these are questions and verses to discuss. You will find that you learn more if you are sharing with others.

At the end of each chapter, you'll have a chance to write at least one thing you want to take away from that chapter on the *Snapshots* pages (at the back of the book). This can include your personal highlights and your action list, so you have in one place everything you want to remember from the entire book.

Study this book with a small group or at least one other person. We highly recommend this. Read through the pages on small groups for suggestions, in the Appendix. Each person should follow the suggestions below for studying alone. Use the questions at the end of each chapter.

Study it alone. The following are some things to consider:
1. Make a commitment to seriously study this book. It is easy to let "more urgent" things crowd out time for study.
2. Find someone who will hold you accountable in your study.
3. Look up each of the verses and meditate on them. We challenge you to memorize some of the verses that stand out to you.
4. Consider studying this book in your personal devotions. It's based on the Word so it makes a great Bible study.

Attend Relationship Resources' *All Stressed Up and Everywhere to Go* **Workshop**. You will gain the most from this book if you study it on your own first, and then attend one of RRI's practical, Biblical, interactive workshops. Contact RRI for a workshop near you or to sponsor one.

When should you use the strategies in this book?

- When you are feeling stressed.
- Before you go into a stressful situation. It helps to deal with whatever stress you currently have, as well as building yourself up for the future. That way you have extra reserves no matter what happens.
- *Now!* It's best, if you can, to study and use the principles when you are not feeling overstressed. Then you'll have them as tools to use when difficulties come up.

Part One
Investigate the Issues

I'm (Gaylyn) jolted out of a deep sleep as another bomb explodes—this one closer than the rest. Trembling, I whisper, "Wow. That was really close. ... I wonder what blew up this time."

Half an hour later, I am still trying to get back to sleep. Suddenly a gunshot pierces the air within a block of our apartment in Guatemala City. I wonder if we're safe. Shifting my position, I pray for our safety.

Tonight is no different from many nights in the past few months. Still, every time a bomb explodes or gunshots blast, I shudder. The guerillas are angry because their candidate didn't become president.

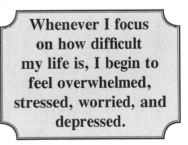

Whenever I focus on how difficult my life is, I begin to feel overwhelmed, stressed, worried, and depressed.

The next morning, dark clouds hang ominously outside our window. At breakfast, my husband and I discuss what we should do. We believed God called us to serve Him here in Central America. Had we misunderstood? Are we supposed to leave? Our work isn't finished and we don't want to flee this beautiful country. But is it safe to stay?

The next day we receive news that Chet Bitterman, a missionary friend in Colombia, South America, had been murdered. Forty-eight days earlier, he was captured and held by terrorists. I remember Chet's amazing love for the Lord during our training with Wycliffe Bible Translators in Dallas, Texas a few years before.

We grieve Chet's death and agonize for his wife and two little girls. Eventually I had to ask, "What if something like that happens to us?"

We arrived in Guatemala in 1979, two years earlier, eager to learn the spoken language of a remote Mayan people group. Our desire was to create a written version of their beautiful language so one day they could read God's Word in their own tongue. I knew this kind of life wouldn't be easy, but I never thought we'd fear for our lives.

The day we learned of Chet's death, I realized I had a choice about how much I would let the stress of that situation affect me. I could become obsessed with the bombs and the danger, or I could focus on God. Focused on the problems around us, I would have packed my bags. Instead, I made the choice to trust God and stay in that war-torn country—even knowing the next bomb might hit our little apartment.

Stress is a normal part of life. I could have been overwhelmed by stress, if I had focused on the gravity of our situation or on all the "what ifs": *What if* I'm captured by terrorists? *What if* either of us gets shot? *What if* a stray bomb hits us? Do you see how this type of thinking could make a stressful situation worse?

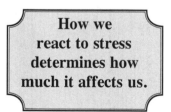

How we react to stress determines how much it affects us.

When problems strike, what do you do? If you're like me, it's easy to only see the pain and difficulties. Although I'll be the first to admit that sometimes pain and difficulties are very real and very present, making them rather difficult to overlook! And yet, when we focus on our problems we can find ourselves blinded to opportunities and blessings, which are also very real and very present, even if they seem eclipsed at the moment.

More often than not, focusing on stress, pain and chaos in our lives creates even *more* stress, pain and chaos for us.

Here's what I've experienced, and my guess is that it's happened to you as well: Whenever I am focused on how difficult my life is, I begin to feel overwhelmed, stressed, depressed, and worried. These emotions, in turn, influence my productivity, actions and choices. They may even change my sleeping patterns and compromise my immune system. Sooner or later they begin to interfere with my relationships with family and friends. They even hinder the way I worship or approach God. As these emotions continue to influence how I live, cope, function, and relate to those around me, they can even impact my finances and long-term security.

However, I'm amazed at what happens when I begin to work through my stressful situations by applying God's Word, rather than wallowing in them. Suddenly I find myself experiencing less stress and a greater measure of peace and joy. I'm capable of embracing saner choices. I don't make as many knee-jerk reactions to pain or fear. My relationships feel healthier. I engage in fewer destructive coping strategies that end up costing me financially, spiritually, emotionally, relationally or even physically.

But you may be saying, "Wait a minute. You don't understand what I'm going through. There is nothing I can change about my situation."

You're right. We don't know what you're going through, although we've been through a few stressful situations.

Here are just a few of the stressful situations I've (Gaylyn) experienced. I was sent away to a boarding school when I was just six years old and had to stay there for eight long years—only seeing my parents on vacations and for a day or two when they would pass through town. I helplessly watched my six-month-old son die. I went through an unwanted divorce and raised my rambunctious sons alone for fifteen years. Then my fiancé was killed one month before our wedding date.

As with Gaylyn, I've (Ken) experienced my share of stress. For 48 years my wife Bobbie and I served with Wycliffe Bible Translators. We drove to Guatemala with Gaylyn (22 months old) and her sister Joy (6 months old). After we arrived, we drove 17 hours over indescribably poor roads, then we hiked for four hours to a remote village that was our home for 11 years. For the first 2 years we shared a primitive two-room house with a family of 5 Indians. No electricity, no plumbing, no heat. We learned and analyzed the unwritten Chuj language, translated the New Testament and other literature into Chuj, established a medical and literacy work, founded a Bible Institute, and other projects. Then we traveled to about 25 countries, providing counseling and training for missionaries, often in difficult locations.

Yes, we do understand stress, although our stresses have probably been different than yours. We don't pretend to have all the answers, but this book has some powerful principles to help relieve stress. They have helped us, personally, as well as thousands of people worldwide.

Today's economy has caused people's stress levels to increase exponentially. Not only are individuals pressured by the things that used to be normal, such as family, finances, health, and children. Now people have added stresses induced by the economy, such as:

- Job loss
- Foreclosures
- Divorces
- Talk of the collapse of US dollar
- Children and teens getting killed at school
- Peer pressure, which is greater now than it used to be
- Drug abuse and other addictions

What issues are you dealing with right now? What is stressing you? While things may seem hopeless at times, because of the direction our economy and country seem to be heading, there is great hope in God. Now more than ever, we need skills to help us work through our stress. The good news is God gave us some amazing tools in His Word. We can't change most stress situations, but we can change how they will affect us.

As you go through this study, we are praying that God will minister to you and help you de-stress your life.

Chapter 1

Embrace the truth
What is stress?

I consider that our present sufferings are not worth comparing with the glory that will be revealed in us.

Romans 8:18

Stress affects all of us, and a joyful, productive life depends on having skills for handling it well. God's Word provides the strategies we need to manage stress well.

We can't choose *whether* we'll have stress, but we can choose *how* it affects us. It can either be a curse—and harm us, or it can be a blessing—and we can thrive in the midst of it.

Before we begin working on specific strategies to manage our stress, we need to look at several issues that are necessary for understanding stress.

For the purposes of this book:

- *Stress* is defined as: *Our response as a whole person to any demand.*

- *Stressor* is defined as: *Any demand put on us that causes stress.*

> **Stress affects all of us, and a joyful, productive life depends on having skills for handling it well.**

Please read those definitions again. Often people confuse stress with stressors. Many think that stress is only the stressors we experience. In fact, that is only a small part of our stress.

Secular views, such as Hans Selye's, see stress as only a *physical* response. A biblical perspective on stress views it as affecting the *whole person—*

- spiritually
- emotionally
- physically
- mentally
- socially

Psalm 31:9-11 is a great example, "Be merciful to me, O LORD, for I am in distress; my eyes grow weak with sorrow, my soul and my body with grief. My life is consumed by anguish and my years by groaning; my strength fails because of my affliction, and my bones grow weak. ... I am the utter contempt of my neighbors; I am a dread to my friends."

The Word of God is our best manual on managing stress. Our Creator understands us infinitely better than anyone, and gives us clear instructions on how to survive stress.

Stress is a normal part of life

Stress is normal. Up to a point, it is helpful and healthy. Often we view all stress as negative, when it is—or can be—very positive. An optimum amount of stress stimulates, invigorates and motivates us. Only when we become overwhelmed by it does it become destructive.

I (Gaylyn) was teaching a class on de-stressing one's life at a seminary in Texas. I asked, jokingly, how many of them did *not* have any stress at all in their lives. I often ask that question to show it's normal to experience stress and it doesn't mean we are unspiritual if we have it.

This particular time one couple raised their hands, proudly telling the group that they had absolutely no stress in their lives. Everyone looked at them incredulously. I was dumbfounded, not knowing how to respond.

At the coffee break, I talked to that couple, just getting to know them. I found out their young daughter had just been molested. They also recently had to flee the country where they served as missionaries, because of terrorists. Yet, they said they had no stress. Interesting. It turned out that they believed that if you experienced any stress, then you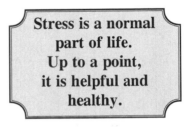

Stress is a normal part of life. Up to a point, it is helpful and healthy.

were not spiritual enough. They were very judgmental of the rest of the group who openly shared their struggles. That couple never did change their thoughts on stress. I'm still not sure why they were in the class.

We want to assure you that you can be spiritual and still experience stress. Jesus, Paul and other biblical characters experienced great stress. They are examples to us of how to handle ours. We will study their stories later.

Biblical Terms

The word "stress" doesn't appear in most Bible translations, although the concept is there throughout. Here are some of the terms used in the Word that mean stress. Look up each verse and write down what you learn from it: (Your translation may use different words than these.)

1. Circumstances—Philippians 4:11
2. Trials—James 1:2; 1 Peter 1:6, 4:12
3. Trouble—John 16:33
4. Hardships—1 Thessalonians 2:9
5. Difficulties—2 Corinthians 12:10
6. Distresses—2 Corinthians 6:4
7. Persecution—John 15:20; 2 Corinthians 12:10;
8. 2 Timothy 3:12
9. Affliction—Job 36:15
10. Suffering—Philippians 1:29; 1 Peter 4:12, 13
11. Pressure—Job 33:7; 2 Corinthians 11:28
12. Discipline—Job 5:17; 1 Corinthians 11:32; Hebrews 12:6

Key Insights about Stress

Note: we will look at each of these points in greater detail throughout the book. As you read through these insights, we encourage you to look up each verse, asking the Lord to reveal what He wants you to learn through them.

1. *The total amount of stress we experience at a given time is cumulative.* Even though there may be no one major cause of stress, the overall load can overwhelm us. Each of us must learn to recognize our own danger signals, and do everything possible to keep stress from going beyond the point of coping.

Secular research has provided an immense amount of data helpful for understanding stress. However, secular views of the effects of stress may be invalid for many Christians. These views see humans as body and mind only, without a

> **The Word encourages us with the fact that heavy stress can actually be constructive for those who resolve it in God's power.**

spirit capable of intimate fellowship with God. This leaves most secular theorists with a pessimistic view of our long-term ability to cope with stress. For example, Hans Selye saw the effects of stress as *inevitably accumulating over time*, so that continued stress will eventually destroy us, no matter what we do. He came to this conclusion based on his experiments with rats!

2. *The effects of stress do accumulate when they are unresolved.* However, most people's experience demonstrates that the cumulative effects of heavy stress are *much less* when the stress is resolved by applying God's resources.

   The Word encourages us with the fact that heavy stress can actually be constructive for those who resolve it in God's power. Stress has the potential of producing more endurance and maturity of character, resulting in greater ability to cope. See Romans 5:3-4 and James 1:2-4.

3. *Spiritual resources provide immeasurable potential for adequately resolving stress.* This is a common theme in the Word. See Isaiah 40:29-31; Matthew 11:28-30 and 2 Corinthians 4:7-18.

4. *We handle stress better in supportive relationships.* See Paul's references to the many helpful people in his life, such as, 2 Timothy 1:16-18.

5. *Even when handled well, stress situations often cause distress.*

Helping Others Handle Stress

One purpose of this book is to give you tools to help others around you to deal with their stress, both adults and children. First, you need to study the principles—and apply them to your own life. Then, learn to recognize the stress in those around you so you can help them identify and effectively handle it.

After you go through each section for yourself, think about your children, your spouse and others close to you. Ask the Lord how you can help them in their situations. You might want to talk with them about this book and see if they would like to go through the study with you.

Sometimes it's easier to recognize stress in adults than it is in children and teens. If you have children, or you work with them, it is very important to learn to identify their stress and how it affects them.

Children and teens are obviously affected by stress, yet consistently parents don't recognize the impact of stress on them. In a recent study by the American Psychological Association, almost half of the teens said they were more worried this past year, yet only about one quarter of their parents said their teen's stress had increased. Very few parents think their children are extremely stressed, yet over a quarter of the teens said they worry "a lot."

Children not only have their own stress, but they also pick up on their parents' stresses. For example, many are worried about their family's financial situations or that their parents might get divorced.

As parents, we have a responsibility to understand our children's stress levels and help them to effectively handle their pressures. You have a great opportunity to give your children the life skills they need in this area. We are both sorry we didn't have these skills to help our children through their stress situations when we were raising them.

Throughout this book, we'll give you specific things you can do to help your children, as well as other children in your life: grandchildren, friend's children, Sunday School kids, and any others.

I (Gaylyn) wish someone had recognized my stress when I was a child at boarding school. I often got stomachaches and was labeled a "hypochondriac." I learned quickly that it wasn't safe for me to tell anyone how I felt. People thought the pain in my stomach was all in my head, that I was making it up to get attention. It wasn't until I was an adult that I began to realize that stomachaches are a symptom my body used to reveal that I was overstressed. In Chapter Five, we'll look at how physical symptoms affect us.

We challenge you not only study these principles for yourself, to make a commitment to help others—but to also children and/or adults—you can be a great blessing as you help them understand and discover solutions to their tensions.

One word of caution as you seek to help others: Take the time to listen to what's going on with the person, rather than just giving advice. Sometimes just allowing someone to talk about their pressures and struggles will help to relieve their stress. Think about this: would you rather have someone give you advice with-out even knowing what the real problem is or would you prefer the person give you an opportunity to talk thru what you're going thru? If you're like most people, it's much more helpful to have someone listen and care.

Recently I (Gaylyn) asked several people to pray for me because I was feeling stressed (ironic isn't it). Rather than discover what I was going through or what I'd done to relieve the pressure, many of them began to give me their advice. It was not the least bit helpful, because it wasn't what I needed, since they didn't know what the issues were.

Questions for personal or group study

1. Consider the definition of stress in this chapter: *Our response as a whole person to any demand*. How does it differ from what you have believed about stress?

2. How can stress be healthy and helpful for you?

3. In what areas are you most overstressed right now? What can—and will—you do about them?

4. Read Hebrews 12:1-3.

   a. What can you learn about handling stress from these verses?

   b. How is Jesus an example for you?

5. Read each of the following verses to discover what resources you have available to resolve your stress. Which will you begin to use today?

   • Isaiah 40:29-31

- Matthew 11:28-30

- 2 Corinthians 4:7-18

- 2 Timothy 1:16-18

6. Look up as many of the Biblical terms, on page 10, as you can. Consider how they apply to you. If you are studying with a group, look them up on your own and write down your insights in the space provided. Then share with the group.

What can I do *today* to lower my stress?

1. Do one thing today to lower your stress, such as sitting down for thirty minutes just to relax or meditate on the Lord. If you're not sure what to do, ask the Lord to show you.

2. Write at least one thing on the *Snapshots* pages (at the end of the book) that you want to remember and/or do. How can you apply it today?

Chapter 2

Recognize the Problem
How Do We Stress Ourselves?

I (Gaylyn) was driving home one evening with my eight-year old, Timothy and we were in the middle of the biggest blizzard I've ever been in—and I've lived in Colorado for sixteen years. By the way, it was mid-October.

Driving down the divided highway, I struggled to see through the almost white-out conditions. As I inched along, suddenly my car began to spin. I found myself doing a 360 degree turn in the middle of the road. Timothy yelled, "Do it again, Mom. Do it again! That was fun." Personally, I was terrified. I like a bit more control in my life!

When we stopped, to my horror, we were on the wrong side of the road, facing the oncoming traffic. It was amazing how God protected us from getting killed that night.

My perception of the situation was totally different than my son's. He had no internal stress to bring to it, so he thought the spinning car ride was a blast. I, on the other hand, could see us getting creamed, like the drunk driver slamming into my car when I was in college.

We had the same stress situation, but totally different reactions, because of our different viewpoints.

The reason two people can have opposite reactions to the exact same situation is because of internal stress—the baggage they bring into the situation.

Let's look at what internal stress is. It is *the burden of unresolved mental and emotional stress we carry with us and bring to new stress situations.*

Often we can't distinguish between the stress caused by external events and the stress we already have within us. We tend to think it always comes from outside of us. The truth is that *most* of our stress comes from inside of us. It can easily make up more than half of the total pressure experienced in a difficult situation.

Unrealistic expectations, destructive attitudes and sore spots can all affect the total amount of stress we feel. While there are many types of internal stress, let's look these three.

Types of Internal Stress

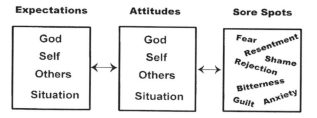

Interaction of different kinds of internal stress

1. **Unrealistic expectations**. A common cause of stress comes from unmet unrealistic expectations. This is especially true if we hold onto them too tightly and aren't willing to let go. They

may be directed toward God, ourselves, others, or situations. Luke 24:21 is a good example: "But we had hoped that he was the one who was going to redeem Israel. And what is more, it is the third day since all this took place."

2. **Destructive attitudes**. Attitudes are *habit patterns of thinking and feeling*. They may be directed toward God, ourselves, others or situations.

Mark 10:13 reveals the disciples' attitude toward children: "People were bringing little children to Jesus to have him touch them, but the disciples rebuked them." They viewed children as a nuisance—just one more stress in their busy lives.

> **Internal stress is:
> The burden of
> unresolved mental and
> emotional stress we carry
> with us and bring to new
> stress situations.**

In the *Questions for Personal or Group Study* we'll look at Exodus 3:10-4:17 to see how Moses' attitudes toward *God*, *himself*, *others* and the *situation* not only brought him intense stress, but also God's anger. Plus, we wonder how many more blessings he missed because of his fears and other destructive attitudes.

Destructive attitudes are often:
- self-perpetuating: we're reluctant to let go of them.

- contagious: we infect others with our attitudes.

- unconscious: often we aren't even aware of them.

- self-deceiving: we sometimes think the problem is external when our attitude is the real problem.

3. **Sore spots**. Sore spots are *emotional wounds that have never healed*. They are like a festering wound; a little pressure can cause a lot of pain. They are the griefs, sorrows, hurts, fears, resentments, or guilt issues that have yet to be resolved through Christ's healing power.

Consider the following facts about sore spots:

- We may or may not be aware of them.

- If they aren't healed, they fester and tend to spread far beyond the original pain.

- Sore spots can cause terrible internal stress, making it difficult to handle external stress. Proverbs 15:13 illustrates this, "A happy heart makes the face cheerful, but heartache crushes the spirit."

4. **Other kinds of internal stress**. We all stress ourselves in various ways. Consider other ways you stress yourself. For example, you might say "I stress myself by constantly thinking that the worst might happen."

Interaction between Types

All types of internal stress interact with each other in complex ways. Each *affects* and is *affected by* the other. For example, unrealistic expectations may cause destructive attitudes, which may cause unresolved emotional pain, which may cause destructive attitudes, and so on.

Look at Paul's internal stress in 2 Corinthians 11:28, "Besides everything else, I face daily *the pressure of my concern* for all the churches" (italics added for emphasis).

Let me (Gaylyn) give you an example from my own life when I experienced overwhelming stress; much of it was internal.

I awoke out of a deep sleep with a start at 12:03 a.m. *What's all that noise?* I heard loud banging on my front door, moving to my living room windows. *What should I do? I can't think straight.* My foggy brain tried to shake off the effects of being awakened from a sound sleep. I was terrified someone had come to hurt me and my boys.

Trembling with fright as the banging continued, I ran to call the police. The phone was dead. Then I remembered I had left the phone off the hook the night before so I could get some peace and sleep. Unfortunately that phone was downstairs in my kitchen.

I started down the stairs, when a bright light suddenly shone in one of my living room windows. The persistent banging got louder. I sat on the stairs shaking violently, trying to decide what to do. *If I try to get to the kitchen, I might be seen and maybe even shot.* "God, I need your help. Please give me wisdom to know what to do," I whispered.

Finally, taking a deep breath, trying to calm my shattered nerves, I sprinted for the phone. *Phew! I made it.* After putting the phone on the hook, I dashed back upstairs, undetected.

As I dialed 9-1-1, I peeked out my bedroom window. *Hmmmm. I wonder why a police car is sitting across the street.* In my fear, it didn't dawn on me.

"9-1-1, what's your emergency?"

Breathlessly, the words tumbled out, "Help me. Someone's banging on my door and shining a bright light in my windows."

I heard the officer on the other end of the line say, "The police are at your house right now."

"What?" My hazy brain tried to grasp what she said. Then a relief began to settle on me.

After hanging up, I went downstairs to open the door. Two officers asked my name and said they had gotten a report I was planning to kill my sons and then myself. Once they started talking to me, they realized I was not suicidal or homicidal, but only extremely shaken.

They still had to go upstairs to check on the boys. One officer shone his bright light into each of my sons' faces, until he could verify they were breathing. I was grateful they were sound sleepers. As I walked the officers to the door, my heart rate finally began returning to normal.

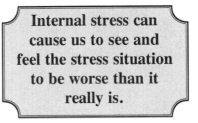

Internal stress can cause us to see and feel the stress situation to be worse than it really is.

This incident was just one more stressor on my already stressful life. It was 1994; just a few months earlier, my life was very different. I was living in Minnesota with my husband, writing books, leading a Bible study on joy, and raising my sons.

Things changed. Now I was in Colorado, a single mom to two rambunctious boys. Suddenly, not only was I a mother and homemaker, I was also responsible for caring for my house, yard and car, bringing in income and raising my sons alone. I was overwhelmed. Saying I was stressed would be a great understatement. I often wondered, *How can I do everything on my own? It's too much.*

Yes, I had significant stressful situations. But I also caused myself more turmoil because of my internal tension. Let me show you how it affected me during that time, because of my expectations, attitudes and sore spots.

Unrealistic expectations. Besides the external stresses, I had many unrealistic expectations. My biggest ones were toward myself. I thought I should be able to be a *perfect* mother as well as fill the role of a father. I found out that I couldn't do either.

I also assumed that I would always be married. Never, in my wildest imaginations, did I ever think I would have to raise my sons alone; I expected God to keep my family together. These were just the beginning.

Destructive attitudes. My attitudes made my stress worse. I had bad attitudes toward my husband (he should have been there helping me raise our boys); toward God (why didn't He help us keep our marriage together?); and toward women who thought they understood what it meant to be a single mom, just because their husbands were gone for a week.

I often had my own "pity parties." *It's not fair. Grumble. Grumble. I shouldn't have to do this all by myself.* Do you ever have pity parties? They're not the most fun parties to attend.

Sore spots. Remember, sore spots are *emotional wounds that have never healed.* I had many of them that wouldn't be resolved for years to come. Some of them revolved around abandonment issues when I was left at a boarding school. Even though I knew in my head that sending me to boarding school was my missionary parents' only viable option, my heart still hurt many years later—

especially as I saw my own children growing up.

I also felt guilty that I wasn't doing a good enough job raising my boys. I resented that I had all the responsibility for caring for them, with no one to help me.

These are just a few of the internal stresses I experienced during those years. They far outweighed the external, because they magnified the problems, making them seem much worse than they already were. For example, when the police were at my door, I was totally stressed. I was terrified, thinking my children and I were in grave danger when, in fact, we were in no danger at all.

Next let's look at how internal stress can magnify—all out of proportion—what we are feeling.

Internal Stress Distorts Our Perception

Look at the diagram on the next page. People often consider the "stress situation" to be the same as our total stress. Notice the stress situation is often only a small part of our total stress. Our internal stress plays a big part and our perception of the situation acts like a lens that magnifies our total stress.

Perception is a lens through which we view a situation or event. It can be distorted by our view of life, where we are focusing, and by the baggage we bring with us into the situation.

I (Ken) saw the amazing power of distorted perception years ago in Bogota, Colombia. A missionary couple came for counseling one morning. They were going back home, because they saw the situation there as utterly intolerable. The people were unfriendly and closed to the gospel. Traffic was horrible. Noise on their street and exhaust fumes were awful. It was very dangerous, and on and on.

That same morning another couple came to talk about the grief they were experiencing because her mother was very ill, and they had to go home to care

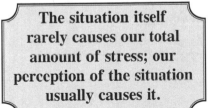

The situation itself rarely causes our total amount of stress; our perception of the situation usually causes it.

for her. They told how much they loved it there; the people were so friendly and open to talk about Jesus. The bus system was great. They felt safe, and much more.

These two couples lived on the same street, a block from each other! Perception determined the lives and careers of these two couples.

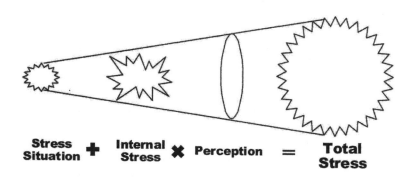

Stress Situation ✚ **Internal Stress** ✖ **Perception** = **Total Stress**

Internal Stress Distorts Our Perception of Reality!

Internal stress dramatically affects our perception of life's situations. The situation itself rarely *causes our total stress*; our *perception* of the situation usually increases it.

Think about my situation with the police:
Stress situation: police pounding on my door
Internal stress: fear, anxiety and expectations that I should have had someone to protect me.
Perception: I was in terrible danger and I might die. My sons might die and it would be my fault, because I can't save them. I'm helpless.
Total stress: I was stressed to the max!

The interaction of unrealistic expectations, destructive attitudes and sore spots distorts our perception of the situation. So we react, not to the situation itself, but to our distorted perception of reality.

In Matthew 26:51-54, when Jesus was arrested, Peter "reached for his sword, drew it out and struck the servant of the high priest, cutting off his ear. 'Put your sword back in its place,' Jesus said to him, 'for all who draw the sword will die by the sword. Do you think I cannot call on my Father, and he will at once put at my disposal more than twelve legions of angels? But how then would the Scriptures be fulfilled that say it must happen in this way?'"

Peter's expectations and attitude caused him to perceive the soldiers who came for Jesus as a threat to the kingdom. He reacted accordingly—drawing his sword to fight for Jesus. Jesus clarified Peter's perception: God is bigger than the situation and could stop it all instantly if He wanted to. However, Jesus could also see the bigger picture: this is what needed to happen for the prophecy to be fulfilled.

Let's look at how internal stress can affect us:
- It can cause us to see and feel the new stress situation to be worse than it really is.

- When seen through our distorted perception, problems are amplified in our minds, and we react, not to reality, but to our distorted view of it.

- Spiritually, mentally, emotionally, and physically we respond as if the situation were worse than it is.

- The illustration on page 24 shows how our internal stress causes us to distort our perception of reality, which in turn magnifies the stress.

Have you ever looked at yourself in the distorted mirrors at an amusement park? One mirror may make you look tall and very thin, while another mirror may make you look short and dumpy. What is the truth? Just because you appear obese, does that make you overweight?

In the same way, your perception of your situation may become distorted by your view of life, which is affected by your internal stress. For example, if your father was always angry and abusive when you were a child, you may view anyone who raises his voice as being angry at you. You may become fearful that the person will become violent. In fact, the man may have just needed to get your attention to warn you that a car was coming and he didn't want you to get hit. But because of your perception of his raised voice, you distort the situation all out of proportion.

Resolving Internal Stress

If you have a personal relationship with Christ, He paid for your sins, but did He take care of all your internal stress? Yes, He *has* taken care of it. He has *already* dealt with all of your pain and struggles. "Surely he took up our infirmities and carried our sorrows" (Isa. 53:4) and "by his wounds you have been healed" (1 Pet. 2:24).

However we must actively trust in what He has done for us. Look up Philippians 3:12-16 and Ephesians 1:15-20 to see what Christ has done for us.

Part of growing requires opening more and more of our lives to God, so that we might experience in reality what He has already done through His life, death and resurrection.

> **All internal stress is a function of the mind, and God's Word clearly provides solutions for it.**

All internal stress is a function of the mind, and God's Word clearly provides solutions for it. Unrealistic expectations and damaging attitudes are resolved through the ongoing, biblical process called *renewing of the mind*. Let's look at it briefly.

1. On the one hand, Christ accomplished everything we need on the cross.

   a. Our old self has *already* been crucified with Him (Rom. 6:1-11).

   b. Colossians 3:10 refers to "the new self, which *is being renewed* in knowledge in the image of its Creator."

2. On the other hand, Ephesians 4:23 commands us continually "to *be made new* in the attitude of your minds." In this way we actively participate in what Christ has done on the cross.

This book is written from a biblical perspective. Many of the principles and skills will help you whether or not you have a personal relationship with God. If you are interested in getting to know God better, turn to Appendix D for more help.

Renewing our minds is an ongoing process.

It is God who continues to make us new, but we are to be involved. This is an active, progressive, life-long process, by which we allow God to bring our inner being into closer and closer conformity to Christ. See Romans 12:1-2: "Do not conform any longer to the pattern of this world, but be transformed by the renewing of your mind."

As we allow God to renew our minds, our *expectations* become more realistic through His knowledge, and our *attitudes* become the very attitudes of Christ. See Philippians 2:1-8.

Are you ready to let go of the hurt and pain you are carrying with you? One of the primary keys to resolving sore spots is forgiveness. Everyone has been hurt in the past, possibly very deeply. It's good to acknowledge the pain. However, holding on to it will only continue to hurt you and can keep you feeling overwhelmed.

Have you ever heard anyone say, or maybe you said it yourself, "I'm not going to forgive so and so, because he doesn't deserve it." You're right. The person probably doesn't deserve it. However, think about this: *Who is continuing to get hurt by your not forgiving the other person? Is he being hurt by your lack of forgiveness? Or are you?*

Second Corinthians 2:10-11 says we are to forgive others "in order that Satan might not outwit us. For we are not unaware of his schemes." One of Satan's schemes is to try to destroy us by our lack of forgiveness. We don't want to give the enemy the power to destroy us, just because we want to hold onto our pain.

Forgiveness is simple, but it's not always easy and it can take time. It's a process. Here are some steps we take, when issues come up, and we have guided many people to wholeness through the same process. Take some time today or in the next few days to do the following:

1. Ask the Lord to reveal your sore spots. You don't need to get back into the hurt, but just be aware of what they are. The pain may seem so obvious that you may not think you need to do this step.

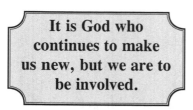

It is God who continues to make us new, but we are to be involved.

2. After you identify each sore spot, ask Him to show you who you need to forgive. There may be numerous people you need to forgive and or many issues with few people.

3. You don't need to go into all the details. Just say something like, "Lord, I forgive _____ for _____ ."

4. That is not the same as saying, "Lord, *help me* to forgive _____ ," although you may need to first ask the Lord for assistance. But then you need to go through the process of forgiving each person for each thing that comes to mind.

5. Keep going through steps 1-3, above, until no more pain comes up.

6. Next, ask God to reveal what lies you may believe, because of your hurt. Stop and listen to what He shows you. The enemy uses our hurts to make us believe lies about God, ourselves, the situation and the other person.

7. Renounce the lies God shows you, in the name of Jesus. For example, if the lie you were believing is that God doesn't care about you, because He allowed the bad things to happen, then you might say, "In the name of Jesus, I renounce the lie that God doesn't care about me." Keep doing this process with each lie the Lord shows you.

8. Then ask the Lord to reveal what the truth is. God loves

revealing truth, but remember to take the time to listen.

You may want to go through this process with a friend. It helps to have someone guiding you. You could give them this list, to help them.

Even if you have forgiven the person or offense before-- and you're sure you're finished forgiving them--if their name or something they did comes up, and you feel the old resentment coming back, you need to forgive again.

There are times when I'm positive I've forgiven someone, but then the hurt and anger come back. I know I still need to do more forgiveness work.

Sometimes you might need help to work through your internal stress. God may lead you to do it alone, relying only on Him. At other times, He will use someone else to help you, such as:

- friends or family members (just be careful that their perception doesn't negatively affect yours, especially if they are too close to the situation)

- your pastor

- a counselor or someone who does some type of healing prayer ministry

If you decide to go to a professional, make sure he comes recommended by someone who *received* help from that person, not just because he is a friend of a friend.

Questions for personal or group study

1. What unrealistic expectations, sore spots and destructive attitudes may be causing you stress today?

   a. Write them out.

   b. What can you do about any of them?

2. Read Numbers 13:1—14:10 for a dramatic example of how internal stress can affect perception.

   a. How did the two spies perceive the situation? How did the other ten perceive it?

   b. How did their perception affect their stress levels?

   c. Notice how contagious a distorted perception is. Apparently, virtually everyone took on the negative, distorted perception of the ten spies. When have you seen this happen?

3. Read Exodus 3:10—4:13.

   a. What do you think Moses missed because of all of his fears and other internal stress?

b. How can you relate to Moses?

c. What can you learn from him?

4. Read each of the following verses. What is the Lord saying to you through each one?

Isaiah 53:4

1 Peter 2:24

Philippians 2:1-8

Philippians 3:12-16

Ephesians 1:15-20; 4:22-24

5. Ephesians 4:32 says, "Be kind and compassionate to one another, forgiving each other, just as in Christ God forgave you." Consider how God forgives you.

a. How can you imitate Him?

b. What's holding you back?

What can I do *today* to lower my stress?

1. Take a few minutes and consider your perception of your present situation. Think about the things that are causing you stress.

   a. Which ones do you think you might perceive as worse than they actually are?

   b. What unrealistic expectations, negative attitudes, sore spots or other internal stress may be distorting your perception?

   Note: Many times we are blind to our own internal stress. Ask the Lord to help you see what may affect you. It helps to discuss your perceptions with someone you trust, asking him to tell you what he sees.

2. List any internal stresses you want to begin working on. Keep these in mind as you consider ways to resolve your internal stress.

3. If you are struggling with sore spots, you might want to skip ahead to Chapter 10 on "Healing in 2 Corinthians."

4. Write at least one thing on the *Snapshots* pages (at the end of the book) that you want to remember and/or do. How can you apply it today?

How can I help others?

1. Consider what internal stresses may be affecting your spouse or friends. You might want to tell about an internal stress you've identified, to give them ideas and encouragement to consider their own. You may also want to share what you're learning from this study.

2. Children normally express their internal stress in disguised ways. Their most common way is to over-react emotionally to small stressors or even unrelated objects or people. Reactions may include anger, temper tantrums, unrealistic fears, aggressive behavior, withdrawal—almost any inappropriate response. If you determine that their reactions are not the problem, but a symptom, you can try to draw them out to discover what is going on. Then you can help them deal with their stress.

3. By the time a child is about 6 years old, you can begin talking about internal stress so they can recognize and name what they are experiencing. Share some of your own so they get the idea, and see that it's okay. For example, "I was really worried that I wouldn't be able to get here for your ball game. But now I see that I worried about nothing, and that made me feel stressed."

Chapter 3

Prevent Burnout
Are You At Risk?

One of the most serious consequences of not adequately dealing with stress is burnout. It is caused by the accumulation of chronic stress that depletes energies. Those who are responsible to care for others and those who hold a strong commitment to serve God are in particular danger, although it can affect anyone.

Burnout is extreme mental, spiritual and/or physical energy exhaustion caused by chronic, unrelieved stress.

We've heard people say, "I'd rather burn out than rust out." Think about that saying. Either way you are out. Personally, we want to live our lives to the fullest to the very end. We don't want to be out of the game of life—either by rusting out or burning out.

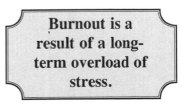

Burnout is a result of a long-term overload of stress.

Dr. Wendell Friest, a psychologist for many years in Taiwan, says about burnout, "The word is borrowed from rocketry science and refers to the point at which the fuel of a missile is completely expended. Using the conception of the term, I don't think it is God's will that any of us 'burn out' during the days of our journey on earth."*

Richard Swenson says, "When stress is pushed to the extremes, burnout results. Next time you go into a forest, take a small sapling and bend it over. When you let go, the tree will straighten back up again. Now take the same sapling and bend it until it breaks. When you let go, it cannot straighten back up.

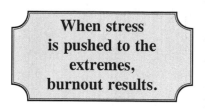

When stress is pushed to the extremes, burnout results.

"This is a picture of burnout. In the same way, in our lives, we adapt and adapt and adapt—and then something inside of us snaps. When this happens, healing comes slowly. I personally do not believe we ever get back the same level of enthusiasm, innocence and passion that we previously had. Yes, there is life after burnout. But most of the healing is by scar formation."**

We can experience spiritual, emotional or physical burnout. Emotional and spiritual burnout often leads to physical burnout. Once a person gets to the state of burnout, it will take much longer to return to normal, than if the individual began working on it earlier.

Causes of Burnout

These are just a few of the causes:

1. High amounts of (or prolonged) stress

2. Too much work

3. Caring for others

4. Becoming overwhelmed by daily routine

5. Unrealistically high expectations from yourself or others

6. Too little sleep

7. Not enough social interaction

8. Not feeling supported in work or home life

9. Too little free time

10. Perfectionist tendencies

Symptoms of Burnout

Here are some common symptoms of burnout. Not every person experiences every symptom. One difficulty in diagnosing burnout is because it is often the beginning stage of (or accompanied by) severe depression. A depressed person will normally demonstrate most or even all of these symptoms.

1. Severe fatigue and irritability

2. Loss of satisfaction in work or ministry

3. Feelings of failure (whether accurate or not)

4. Sleep disturbances (any kind)

5. Difficulty handling people problems

6. Difficulty making decisions

7. Blaming others for problems

8. Feelings of hopelessness and being trapped in the job, ministry or relationship

9. Feeling guilty much of the time

10. Feeling inadequate, alone, empty, disillusioned, exhausted, unenthusiastic, or ineffective

11. Emotional exhaustion

12. Pessimistic outlook

13. Lowered immunity to physical illnesses

14. Sense of emptiness and depletion

15. Desire to leave work or home and never come back

16. Little or no joy in work, ministry and/or other activities

17. Concern about not being able to go on

18. Relating to people becomes more and more difficult

19. Feelings of dread about adequately fulfilling obligations

20. Cynicism

21. Loss of eternal perspective

22. Desire for life to be over

23. Heightened anxiety

24. Strained relationships

Burnout Inventory

These questions may give you an idea to what degree you are experiencing burnout.

Rate your response to each question from 1 to 5.
I experience this...
1 = never, 2 = occasionally, 3 = fairly often,
4 = most of the time, 5 = nearly all the time

_____ 1. I am exhausted most of the time, and rest does not help much.

_____ 2. I do not get as much satisfaction out of my relationships and activities as I used to.

_____ 3. I dread getting up most mornings.

_____ 4. I often feel like a failure in what I'm doing.

_____ 5. I do not sleep as well as I used to.

_____ 6. It is more and more difficult for me to deal with people's problems.

_____ 7. I have more difficulty making decisions than I used to.

_____ 8. I get very frustrated when things don't go well.

_____ 9. More and more I find myself "just hanging on" until I can get out of this responsibility.

_____ 10. My feelings of guilt over work that is not done or not done well bothers me greatly.

_____ 11. I get angry and/or irritable more easily than I used to.

_____ 12. I often feel a sense of emptiness and depletion, like I have nothing more to give.

_____ 13. My work and other activities give me very little or no joy.

_____ 14. I am concerned I won't be able to last much longer fulfilling my obligations.

_____ 15. It is getting more and more difficult to live up to all that is expected of me by everyone.

_____ **Total**

> *15-29:* *You probably don't have a problem with burnout.*
>
> *30-49:* *You may be experiencing mild to moderate burnout.*
>
> *50-64:* *You may be suffering significant burnout.*
>
> *65-75:* *You may be in serious trouble!*

Here is one of our best secrets for avoiding burnout. **It could be the most important skill you can develop to keep out of trouble.**

It's very simple: **learn how to say a "prayerful no."** For example, if you are asked to take on a significant new responsibility (and you have the option to say no) take these steps: Tell the person you want to pray about it before making a decision. The greater the commitment of time and energy, the longer you may need to pray and weigh the pros and cons. As you seek God's guidance, do the following:

1. Ask yourself hard questions, such as:

    a. How would doing this benefit others, the Kingdom of God, myself, or my family?

    b. How would it negatively impact others, myself or my family?

    c. Am I the only one who can do it?

    d. How much time and energy will it take? (Magnify your estimate by three!)

    e. How well am I coping with my current responsibilities?

    f. What will I *stop* doing if I do this?

    g. Will adding this responsibility bring greater love, joy and peace?

2. Get counsel from those close to you, especially those who will be affected by your decision.

3. If in doubt after going through this process, it is usually wise to say "no."

All this may sound very self-centered, but sometimes the most spiritual thing you can do is to say "no" to some very good activities. If you burn out, you will not be any good for God, your family, your ministry, yourself, or anyone else.

What can you do if you are in—or on the verge of—burnout?

Here are a few ideas to get you started:

1. Begin applying your "best strategy" *immediately*.

2. Take some time off from work or ministry if at all possible. You will end up more effective. During that time, allow yourself to:

    a. Rest and sleep, without feeling guilty. Read the section on rest in Chapter 11.

    b. Spend time alone with the Lord.

    c. Do some things you enjoy doing.

    d. Examine and let go of your unrealistic expectations of yourself and the expectations others have of you.

    e. Do the exercises in this book to learn how to manage your stress so you don't get worse.

    f. Find a friend, pastor or counselor to help you work through the issues that affect you the most.

If you are truly burned out, an extended time off will probably be needed for healing.

Note: If you are seriously burned out, with clear symptoms of depression, seek professional help as soon as possible.

Questions for personal or group study

1. As you read the list of symptoms of burnout, can you relate to any of them? Which ones?

2. How did you do on the *Burnout Inventory*? What will you do to lower your score?

3. How could the following verses help you avoid burnout?

    Psalm 28:7

    Psalm 55:22

    Psalm 103:1-5

    Psalm 130:5-7

    Isaiah 26:3

    Matthew 11:28-30

    John 14:27

    Philippians 4:6-9

Hebrews 12:1-3

4. What can you learn from the following Bible characters?
   - Moses: Exodus 18:13-27

   - Elijah: 1 Kings 17-19, especially chapter 19, but chapters 17-18 give background for Elijah's burnout.

What can I do *today* to lower my stress?

1. As you look through this chapter, what things do you need to do so that you don't burn out?

2. If you scored 50 or higher on the "Burnout Inventory," find someone who can help you lower your stress. Don't wait. You need to do something soon, so you don't burn out completely.

3. Write at least one thing on the *Snapshots* pages (at the end of the book) that you want to remember and/or do. How can you apply it today?

How can I help others?

1. Look at the people around you, including children. Do any of them show any of the signs of burnout? If so, ask the Lord to show you what you can do to help them. It may be offering to help with their workload or just letting them talk.

2. If you believe any of them are in burnout or close to it, you might want to ask them if they want to take the burnout inventory, and then discuss the results with them.

3. You can offer to be a sounding board for them to talk about how they feel. You can encourage them to study this book with you. But remember that they may need some professional help.

4. The greatest thing you can do for people is to pray for them. We've found that most people won't turn you down, if you offer to pray for them. It can be very encouraging to hear someone else praying out loud, as well as knowing you'll continue to pray.

    We often go out to breakfast together, as Dad and Daughter. When the server brings our meal, we say, "We're going to thank God for our food. How can we pray for you?" Not one person has reacted negatively. In fact, most give a thoughtful (and sometimes heart-breaking) request.

---

* http://www.tmf.org

** Richard A. Swenson. *The Overload Syndrome,* ©1998. Used by permission of NavPress Publishing. All rights reserved. For copies of the book call 800-366-7788.

Part Two
De-Stress Your Life

*To this you were called,
because Christ suffered for you,
leaving you an example
that you should follow in his steps.*
1 Peter 2:21

This part of the book is filled with very practical skills you can use now and throughout your life to lower your stress. They are simple, yet very powerful, and can be used in any situations. It's important to go through each one, in order, because they build on each other.

We have both taught these skills worldwide for years, and we continue to apply them in our lives. For example, just a few weeks ago, I (Gaylyn) was feeling overstressed. Hey, writing a book on stress is bound to stress me, right? I must say, that wasn't all that was going on in my life at the time.

I've learned I don't have to allow difficult situations to overwhelm me, although I forget sometimes. When I do, I can begin to feel crushed under the weight of it all. And, as you've probably experienced, that's not a very nice feeling.

I decided I better practice what I was "preaching." I went through each of the skills in this section of the book, and it was amazing how my stress level reduced.

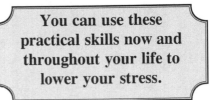

You can use these practical skills now and throughout your life to lower your stress.

reduced. Nothing outward changed in my life, yet my stress went down. Would you like be able to do that? Keep reading.

Just like any new skill, it may seem cumbersome at first, but as you practice it gets easier. Recently when I went through the process, it only took about an hour to go through all six skills. But it was an hour well spent, because afterward I was able to accomplish more in less time, with less stress.

We have both seen the power in these skills, firsthand in our own lives, as well as in other people's lives. We pray God will do some amazing things in your life as you learn them and apply them.

Here is an overview of the six important skills in managing your stress that you'll study in the next few chapters.

Skill 1: Determine Your Stressors: What's causing your stress?

Skill 2: Understand Your Reactions: How is it affecting you?

Skill 3: Stop the Pain: How do you handle your emotions?

Skill 4: Harness Your Resources: How can you enlist God's help?

Skill 5: Relieve the Pressure: How can you lower your stress?

Skill 6: Transform Your Circumstances: How will focusing on God help you?

Jesus, our model

Jesus is our example for how to manage stress effectively. He experienced an incredible amount of stress for our sake, and yet He endured. He didn't give up. He didn't let it overwhelm Him.

As 1 Peter 2:21 says, we are to follow His example, not only by suffering, but also by handling suffering (or stress) like He did.

Isaiah 53 describes Jesus as:
- a man of sorrows
- familiar with suffering
- despised
- rejected
- pierced
- crushed
- wounded

- oppressed
- afflicted

Yes, Jesus knew all about stress. Any one of the above descriptions would cause us intense stress.

As we examine and practice each of the six skills, we'll consider how Jesus applied them in His life, especially as He went to the cross. As we follow His example we learn to effectively handle stress as He did.

Remember, this book, won't help you if you just read it. It is a workbook for you to study each skill now, as well as to have the skills so you can use them in the future.

Here are some times and ways you can use these skills:
- Work through the steps whenever you are feeling over-stressed.

- These skills can also help you when you *anticipate* going into a stressful situation. You can deal with the stresses in your life *before* you go into the new situation, so that you don't make the situation worse.

- You can also use these skills to help others, when you see them going through very stressful situations, or when they seem overstressed, but don't *appear* to have major issues in their lives.

Chapter 4

Determine Your Stressors
What is causing your stress?

The first skill in handling stress is to identify what's causing it. We can't begin to manage our stress unless we know what the specific causes are.

What if you went to a doctor and told him, "I feel terrible but I don't want to tell you what's wrong. Just do something to heal me." How much could he help you? He may laugh at you (although he probably wouldn't show it). Yet how often do we do something similar? We just want to get rid of our stress, but we don't want to carefully consider what the causes are.

Just as a doctor must know what's wrong before he can help us, so too we must first know what is causing our stress, before we can "fix" it.

As we go through each skill, we'll look at Jesus as our example. Jesus boldly faced His most appalling stress situation—going to the cross, taking our sins on Himself—and He clearly identified its causes. We'll look at a few examples at the end of this chapter in *Questions for personal or group study*.

Some General Sources of Stress
Internal

- Health
- Spiritual struggles
- Emotional struggles
- Life stages
- Unrealistic expectations
- Negative attitudes
- Emotional pain
- Anxiety over the future

External

- Marriage and family
- Major changes
- Difficult relationships
- Living situation
- Work/ministry situation
- Unsettled future
- Financial problems
- The economy
- Spiritual warfare
- Add some of your own

Spiritual warfare is not a source of stress we often consider, yet it is very real. We have an enemy who "prowls around like a roaring lion looking for someone to devour." (1 Pet. 5:8). This is rarely, if ever, the only cause of our stress, but he can use our other sources of stress to make them worse.

We need to recognize that Satan has a plan for our lives. He comes to steal, kill and destroy, according to John 10:10. We must stand against him and not allow him to steal our joy (or anything else) to kill our ministry or destroy our family.

What can I do *today* to lower my stress?

This process is essential to getting the most out this book.

1. On a separate sheet begin to list the specific causes of stress in your life over the past six months. See the *General Sources of Stress* above, to give you ideas—for example, "health." Don't just write "health" on your list. Write each specific health issue you are dealing with. Remember that not all causes of stress are negative. For example, the following events may—probably will—cause you stress:

   - Getting married (you have to adjust to living with someone new)

   - Having a baby (they cry, wake up at all hours of the night and make messes)

   - Going on vacation (it brings changes to your routine and living situation)

2. Then rate each one with a number from 1 and 10 to indicate how much stress it is causing. For example, 1 means it's hardly noticeable; 5 means it really gets my attention; and 10 says I can't tolerate it if there's no relief immediately!

   Keep your list so you can review and add to as you continue to study stress. This will help you apply the principles to your situation.

   NOTE: You may be feeling more stress now than you were when you started this chapter. Remember, this process doesn't *cause* the stress. It only brings it out in the open so you can work on it. If you're like many people, you may not realize why you're feeling stressed until you do this step.

I (Gaylyn) remember one time going through this process when I was feeling very stressed, but couldn't understand why it was so overwhelming. As I wrote down everything that was affecting me at the time, I started to cry. I could clearly see why I felt inundated. It was a relief to know there was a reason I felt the way I did.

3. Go over your list of stressors with your spouse or a good friend, and discuss the following questions:

    a. How is each stressor affecting me personally and us together?

    b. Which are we both experiencing?

    c. Which stressors are one of us experiencing but not the other?

    d. Which ones can we begin doing something about individually or together?

    e. What specifically will we begin doing today?

4. Write at least one thing on the *Snapshots* pages (at the end of the book) that you want to remember and/or do. How can you apply it today?

Questions for personal or group study

1. What did you learn as you listed your stressors? If you didn't do the project, please go back and do it now. The rest of this book is dependent on your doing this first skill.

2. Consider the following passages to see how Jesus faced His terrible stress situation and how He clearly identified its causes. Write what you learn from each.

   Matthew 26:20-24: "And while they were eating, he said, 'I tell you the truth, one of you will betray me.'"

   Matthew 26:38: "My soul is overwhelmed with sorrow to the point of death."

   Mark 14:27-30: "You will all fall away," Jesus told them, "for it is written: 'I will strike the shepherd, and the sheep will be scattered....tonight—before the rooster crows twice you yourself will disown me three times."

Luke 22:37: "It is written: 'And he was numbered with the transgressors'; and I tell you that this must be fulfilled in me. Yes, what is written about me is reaching its fulfillment."

How can I help others?

1. With adults and teens:
    a. Encourage them to list each of their stressors. They might need your help to identify some they don't recognize.
    b. Then have them rate each one on a scale of 1-10.

2. Teens and tweens today are under a lot of stress at school and/ or work, in the community, with friends, in broken homes, etc. This exercise can empower them to handle their situations better. It will also give them practical tools they need throughout their lives. I (Gaylyn) took my sons through these principles when they were teenagers.

3. With children, ask them to talk about what kinds of things are bothering them. Depending on their ages, you might be able to get them to talk about how much stress they are under, how they feel, how it affects them, etc. Use words they will understand in place of stress, such as, "bad feelings" or "things that don't go the way you want." As you go through this book you will learn more how to help them resolve their stress.

Chapter 5

Understand Your Reactions
How is stress affecting you?

Everyone develops some healthy and unhealthy reactions to stress. Whether a reaction is healthy or not often depends on how it is handled. Some reactions are inherently more destructive than others.

This section will help you better understand *how* you react to particular stress situations, and *why* you react as you do. As you gain insight you can become more effective in making choices to cope better at each point in the process.

General Effects of Stress

To determine how you are reacting to stress, it helps to determine the total amount of stress you are experiencing. Look at the figure below to help you understand your stress.

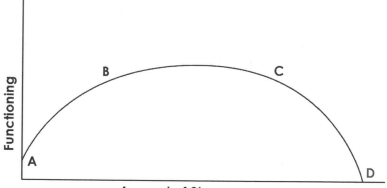

Amount of Stress

In the figure above:

- The left side shows how healthy we are in our relationships, ministry and lives—spiritually, physically, mentally, and emotionally.

- The bottom line shows how much stress we have in our lives: the left side, point "A," is extremely low stress, the right side, point "D," designates extreme stress.

- Notice that at first, as stress goes up, our well-being improves. We need some stress for physical, emotional and spiritual health.

- It is impossible to have no stress, because zero stress is to be dead. Many people want to get rid of all their stress, but we need some stress to be able to live well.

- Between Points B and C we have an optimal amount of stress. Here is the best place to live, with enough stress to keep us at or near peak well-being. Each of us needs to figure out where our Point B and C is. Ask yourself, "What is my optimal amount of stress, so that I have maximum well-being?"

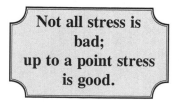

Not all stress is bad; up to a point stress is good.

- We can go past Point C for short

periods, and need to be willing to do so from time to time. However, problems come when we are living past C for weeks, months or even years. Some people think that the more spiritual you are the more stress you can endure. That's not necessarily true. We need to figure out how we can best glorify God in our lives. Living consistently on overload is rarely, if ever, the way to do it.

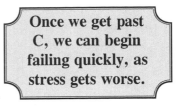

> Once we get past C, we can begin failing quickly, as stress gets worse.

- The total amount of stress in our lives is almost always made up of many sources. Rarely does one major stressor cause us to go past C.

- At point D we have so much stress we are no longer functioning. I (Ken) have counseled many missionaries who have had to abandon their calling because the constant unrelenting stress brought them to a point of total physical, mental and spiritual exhaustion. Some never fully recovered.

- When we get past C, most of us begin failing more and more dramatically as our stress gets worse. This is because we are living on our reserves, and depleting them faster than we can replenish them. It is also at this point where we begin to lose perspective, insight and wisdom.

- The curve, on the previous page, is an average of many people. However, just as God made each of us unique, we are also each distinct in our innate capacity to cope with stress, for example:

- Some people have a very long curve that appears to keep going up no matter how much stress they encounter. See the next diagram. They can handle massive amounts of stress without serious problems. However, everyone has a point when they will begin to go downhill.

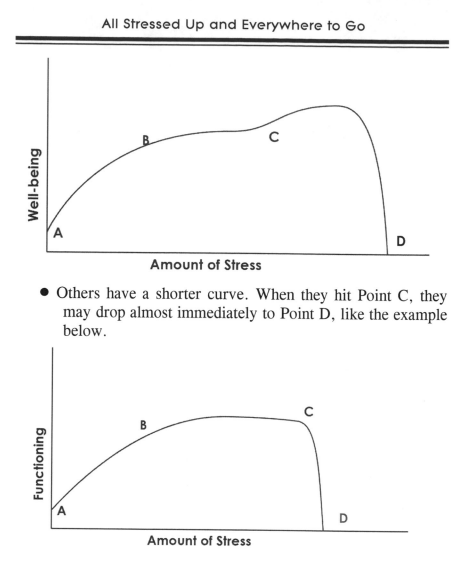

- Others have a shorter curve. When they hit Point C, they may drop almost immediately to Point D, like the example below.

We must not judge others in this, or think that our curve is a measure of our spirituality. We need to accept both ourselves and others in how God created us. Let's discern where *we* best function, and give others grace to be who God created *them* to be.

We knew a missionary couple—Bible translators—who *seemed* to live between Points A and B. Other missionaries criticized them and even made fun of them: they walked slowly, they drove slowly, they talked slowly, and they worked slowly. They did everything seemingly in slow motion. Yet, while other missionaries had burned out and left the mission field, this couple kept going strong, serving God faithfully for over sixty years. Sixty years! And instead of just translating *one* New Testament, like others did, they translated *five!*

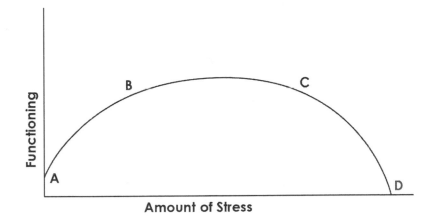

Amount of Stress

Reflect

1. Reflect, and mark on the curve below, where you think you are right now on the curve.

    Where were you three months ago?

    Where were you six months ago?
    Ask your spouse or another person close to you where he thinks you are.

2. If the trend continues without change, where will you be in six months?

Specific Effects of Stress
Symptom Reactions

Once we have estimated our total amount of stress, we need to consider what, if any, symptoms of stress we are experiencing.

**Symptoms are *potentially destructive reactions
when we aren't coping well with stress.***

Sometimes symptoms aren't easily identified with the source of stress. They are usually ineffective attempts by the mind and body to reduce stress by *detouring* it elsewhere. For example, one may develop stomach pain when under time pressure. Our symptoms can change over time.

Symptoms may be *friends or foes*, depending on what we do with them. They are friends if we heed them as danger signals, and are motivated by them to work on managing the stress better. They become enemies, foes, if we ignore them and allow them to harm us.

A few years ago, I (Gaylyn) was under an excessive amount of stress: running a business and a ministry, raising my sons alone, and dealing with some major challenges with one of my sons. I began to experience chest pains that became more severe and frequent. Even though I was *almost* positive they were due to my tension levels, I still went to my doctor. I told her my symptoms, but also explained I thought they were probably just from anxiety.

She ran a series of tests on my heart, just to rule out any physical problems. There were a few abnormalities, but nothing to explain the pain I was feeling. That confirmed I needed to reduce my stress. So I went through these six skills to de-stress my life. They helped me to lower my stress levels.

> *Symptoms may be friends or foes, depending on what we do with them.*

It's important to get any potentially serious symptoms checked with a doctor. At the same time, you can begin to work through these skills.

Kinds of Symptoms

Psalm 139 and other Scriptures emphasize our complexity. This may be seen in the diversity of symptoms we produce when we aren't coping well with stress.

Each of us develops our own unique combination of symptoms, depending on the amount and type of stress we're experiencing. Symptoms occur on a continuum from external to internal kinds.

1. *External symptoms.* These symptoms attempt to detour stress and its distress *outward*, away from ourselves, to seek relief.

   a. They are usually *fight or flight* reactions, usually directed at objects and persons *unrelated* to the source of the stress. An example is a father who comes home from an especially hard day at work and either yells at his wife and children or escapes to his bedroom.

   b. They fail to help and often have destructive consequences which produce *more* stress.

   c. They may also lead us into sinful behavior and attitudes. The Israelites' rebellion and Moses' anger toward God recorded in Numbers 11:1-15 illustrate external symptoms of stress. You'll have a chance to study these verses later in the chapter.

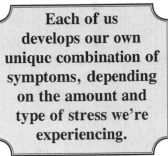

> Each of us develops our own unique combination of symptoms, depending on the amount and type of stress we're experiencing.

   See *A Checklist of Stress Symptoms* on the following pages for examples of a few common external symptoms.

2. *Internal symptoms.*

   a. These attempt to detour stress and its distress *inward*, and may be spiritual, emotional or physical in nature. Stress headaches are a common example. Early in our marriage, I (Ken) was taking a full load at University of California Berkley, working 40 to 48 hours a week, driving three hours a day, and a new baby in our home. But I couldn't understand why I had serious abdominal pain much of the time!

b. Often we aren't aware of what we're doing when we develop these symptoms.

c. They may occur when we bury our distresses, or when the stress is overwhelming. Psalm 22:12-15 illustrates the latter. Look at a few of them:

1) "all my bones are out of joint"

2) "my heart has turned to wax; it has melted away within me"

3) "my strength is dried up like a potsherd"

4) "my tongue sticks to the roof of my mouth"

5) "I can count all my bones"

Symptoms are not necessarily a sign of abnormality or an indication that we are failing to deal with our stress. Sometimes the stress is so great that even when we do everything we can to manage it, we still produce symptoms.

Even Jesus experienced symptoms of stress. "Being in anguish, he prayed more earnestly, and his sweat was like drops of blood falling to the ground" (Luke 22:44).

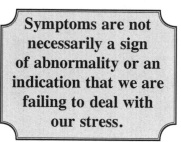

Symptoms are not necessarily a sign of abnormality or an indication that we are failing to deal with our stress.

The American Psychological Association[*] discovered that many adults say they have felt the physical effects of stress in the past month:

- 47 percent say they lay awake at night
- 45 percent are irritable or angry
- 43 percent describe fatigue
- 40 percent convey lack of interest, motivation or energy
- 34 percent have headaches
- 34 percent say they feel depressed or sad
- 27 percent have upset stomachs or indigestion from stress

A Checklist of Stress Symptoms

Please note: All of these symptoms may be the result of causes other than stress. Physical causes should be checked in serious cases. Emotional and spiritual problems can also be at the root of many of these.

Look over this checklist. Reflect on and mark:

a. **What symptoms do you tend to have when you are not coping well?**

b. **Which are you experiencing now, if any?**

c. **Which have you had in the last six months?**

d. **Which are friends and which are enemies?**

Relational Symptoms

Avoiding others
Anger and/or hostility toward unrelated objects and people
Difficulties in resolving conflicts
Critical attitude
Impatience
Insensitivity to others' needs
Intolerance of others
Irritability
Loss of desire for intimacy with God
Rebellion to human authority or even to God
Uncontrolled temper outbursts

Emotional symptoms

Anxiety, with no specific focus
Apathy
Depression
False guilt
Fears that have no basis in reality
Indecision
Nervousness
Overwhelming discouragement
Panic attacks
Psychosis
Self-condemnation
Sense of failure or total inadequacy

Physical symptoms (Often a physical basis exists, but symptoms are much worse because of the stress)

Accident proneness
Allergies
Appetite disturbances
Arthritis
Asthma
Chest pains
Eating disorders
Fatigue
Gastrointestinal distress
Headaches, migraines
Hypertension
Hypoglycemia
Physical pain, especially back, neck and shoulders
Numbness
Memory impairment
Sleep disturbances
Sexual dysfunction
Trembling
You may want to add others of your own to these lists.

What can I do *today* to lower my stress?

1. If you didn't do the section marked, "Reflect" under "General Effects of Stress", take the time to do it now. It is important that you get a good understanding of where you are currently and in what direction you are going.

2. What symptoms are you having now?

   a. Which are affecting you the most?

   b. What is the trend?

   c. What do you need to do about them?

3. Write at least one thing on the *Snapshots* pages (at the end of the book) that you want to remember and/or do. How can you apply it today?

Questions for personal or group study

1. How is stress affecting you overall right now? What does your curve look like?

2. Read Psalm 139. How has God created us each differently?

3. Luke 22:44 says, "And being in anguish, he prayed more earnestly, and his sweat was like drops of blood falling to the ground." What does this say to you about spirituality and stress symptoms?

4. What symptoms do you see in the following verses? Consider what you can learn from each one.
   - Numbers 11:1-15

   - Psalm 32:9-10

   - Psalm 22:12-15

How can I help others?

You can do the following for your children, spouse or friends:

1. Explain the stress curve. Help them estimate where they are and which way they are going on it.

2. Explain stress symptoms. Mention a few of your own, and encourage them to talk about what their symptoms look like when they are overstressed. Tell them that Jesus Himself had symptoms, so it must be okay.

3. Ask yourself, or you might ask the person:

   a. "What stressors seem to be causing these symptoms?"

   b. "What can I begin doing to help them cope better?" Or "what can you begin doing to cope better?

* Stress in America 2009.

Chapter 6

Stop the Pain
How do you handle your emotions?

Be merciful to me, O LORD, for I am in distress;
my eyes grow weak with sorrow,
my soul and my body with grief.

Psalm 31:9

We must lay to rest the myth that if we are truly spiritual we will never be upset or feel emotional pain when under stress. God's Word makes it clear that it is normal to feel distress. Study the lives of Jesus, Paul and David for examples.

The spiritual person *does* feel distress when under intense stress. Consider what Jesus said in Matthew 26:36-38: "Then Jesus went with his disciples to a place called Gethsemane,... and he began to be sorrowful and troubled. Then he said to them, 'My soul is overwhelmed with sorrow to the point of death. Stay here and keep watch with me.'" See also Psalm 6:1-7 and 2 Corinthians 5:2-4.

Here are a few examples of how you may experience distress:

1. Your best friend broke trust by telling others something you shared in confidence. You may feel *angry, sad, hurt, wounded,* and/or *betrayed.*

2. Your computer crashes and you lose all your data. You may feel *frustrated, baffled, dismayed, unhappy,* and/or *furious.*

3. You expected your vacation to be restful, but it seemed like everything went wrong. You may feel *disappointed, discouraged,* and/or *frustrated.*

David often talked about his distresses. Psalm 31:9 is one of many examples, when he wrote, "Be merciful to me, O LORD, for I am in distress..."

One purpose of distress is to drive us to the Lord. Psalm 119:67 says, "Before I was afflicted I went astray, but now I obey your word."

Second Corinthians 1:9 says, "In our hearts we felt the sentence of death. But this happened that we might not rely on ourselves but on God, who raises the dead."

Let's look at the *Distress Checklist,* on the following pages.

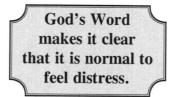

God's Word
makes it clear
that it is normal to
feel distress.

Distress Checklist

Here are some of the distresses experienced by God's people in the Bible. We encourage you to look up each verse and write down what you learn from them.

You may want to rate yourself on how often you experience each distress:
1=rarely or never, 2=occasionally,
3=often, 4=most of the time

1. **Afraid**—Psalm 56:3; Mark 4:40

2. **In agony**—Psalm 6:2

3. **Alarmed**—Psalm 31:22; Mark 16:5

4. **Angry**—Psalm 5:1; Mark 3:5

5. **In anguish**—Psalm 25:1, 6:3; 2 Corinthians 2:4

6. **Anxious**—Psalm 94:19; Proverbs 12:25; Philippians 2:28

7. **Ashamed**—Psalm 4:2, 6:10; 2 Corinthians 9:4

8. **Astonished**—Galatians 1:6

9. **Bewildered**—Isaiah 21:3; Mark 16:8

10. **Burdened**—Matthew 11:28; 2 Corinthians 5:4

11. **Confused**—Galatians 1:7, 5:10

12. **Crushed**—Psalm 10:10; Proverbs 17:20, 18:4

13. **In despair**—Psalm 88:15; 2 Corinthians 1:8

14. **Disgraced**—Psalm 55:2, 69:19

15. **Dismayed**—Psalm 116:11, 143:4

16. **Distraught**—Psalm 55:2

17. **Distressed**—Psalm 69:29, 77:2, 102:2, 107:6, 13, 19; 2 Corinthians 1:6, 2:4, 6:4; Philippians 2:26

18. **Disturbed**—Psalm 42:5, 11; Acts 15:24

19. **Downcast**—Psalm 42:5-6, 11; 2 Corinthians 7:6

20. **In dread**—Psalm 14:5, 110:39

21. **Embittered**—Psalm 73:21

22. **Forlorn**—Psalm 35:2

23. **Frustrated**—2 Samuel 13:2

24. **Grieved**—Psalm 31:9, 73:21; 2 Corinthians 12:21

25. **Hatred**—Psalm 31:6, 139:21-22

26. **Heart wounded**—Psalm 109:22

27. **In Horror**—Psalm 55:5

28. **Hurt**—John 21:17; 2 Corinthians 7:8

29. **Indignant**—2 Corinthians 7:11

30. **Jealous**—2 Corinthians 11:2

31. **Lonely**—Psalm 25:16, 68:6

32. **In mourning**—Psalm 35:14, 38:6

33. **Overwhelmed**—Psalm 55:5; Matthew 26:38

34. **No peace of mind**—2 Corinthians 2:12

35. **Perplexed**—Daniel 4:19; 2 Corinthians 4:8;

Galatians 4:20

36. **Pressured**—2 Corinthians 1:8, 11:28

37. **Regretful**—2 Corinthians 7:8

38. **Sad**—Matthew 26:22; Mark 14:19

39. **Shaken**—Psalm 16:8

40. **Sorrowful**—Psalm 6:7; 2 Corinthians

2:7, 6:10

> **Jesus Himself experienced distress, and this gives us permission to be distressed also!**

41. **Terrified**—Daniel 4:19; Psalm 90:7

42. **Troubled**—Psalm 38:18, 77:4; John 12:27; Acts 16:18

43. **Unsettled**—1 Thessalonians 3:3; 2 Thessalonians 2:2

44. **At Wits End**—Psalm 107:27

45. **Weary**—Psalm 119:28; Matthew 11:28

Jesus' Example

Jesus Himself experienced distress, and this gives us permission to be distressed also. God's Word says that He was...

Angry: **Mark 3:5**
Deeply moved in spirit: **John 11:33, 38**
Distressed: **Mark 14:33**
Afraid (godly fear): **Hebrews 5:7**
Grieved: **Matthew 26:38; Mark 14:34**
Troubled: **Mark 14:33; John 12:27; 11:33**

These terms are all from the RSV.

Jesus handled His distress well. He took the following steps to manage the emotional distress He experienced as He went to the cross. But remember, He still *felt* great emotional pain.

1. He allowed Himself to feel it (Matt. 26:37; John 13:21).

2. He clearly identified it (Matt. 26:38; John 12:27).

3. He expressed His distress (Heb. 5:7).

4. He shared His pain with others (Matt. 26:38).

5. He forgave those who caused His pain (Luke 23:34).

It's encouraging that Jesus experienced distresses. That makes us know we are okay when we feel emotional pain. I (Gaylyn) used to have a close friend who I would call occasionally and say, "I just need to rant and rave!" She would listen as I shared with her what I was feeling. Sometimes I do the same thing with the Lord. He's a great listener and He's always there, even when friends aren't.

Questions for personal or group study

1. What has been your opinion of distress? Many people believe that distress is wrong and unspiritual. If that was your belief, how has that changed from this study?

2. Carefully consider *Jesus' Example* on the previous page.

   a. Notice each distress Jesus felt. Which ones surprise you that Jesus would experience them?

   b. Compare how you handle your distresses with how Jesus handled His. What do you learn from each of the following verses?

      Matthew 26:37-38: "He took Peter and the two sons of Zebedee along with him, and he began to be sorrowful and troubled. Then he said to them, 'My soul is overwhelmed with sorrow to the point of death. Stay here and keep watch with me.'"

      Hebrews 5:7: "During the days of Jesus' life on earth, he offered up prayers and petitions with loud cries and tears to the one who could save him from death, and he was heard because of his reverent submission."

Luke 23:34: "Jesus said, 'Father, forgive them, for they do not know what they are doing.'"

    c. What do you want to do differently to be more like Jesus in these areas?

3. Look up as many of the verses in this chapter as you can. Ask the Lord to show you what He wants you to learn and apply from them.

What can I do *today* to lower my stress?

When you are experiencing significant distress, consider going through these steps:

1. Mark the distresses you are experiencing on the "Distress Checklist."

2. Allow yourself to feel the full force of each distress, as much as you can. This doesn't create pain; it helps let go of it.

3. Take each one to the Lord and express it to Him.

4. Seek to share your distresses with a trusted loved one or friend.

5. Begin working on forgiving anyone who may have brought on your pain. See page 28 for more on forgiveness.

6. Write at least one thing on the *Snapshots* pages (at the end of the book) that you want to remember and/or do. How can you apply it today?

How can I help others?

Each person is different. Be sensitive when you approach friends and family on distresses they may be experiencing. Some have grown up believing that all distress is sin. You might share what you learned about Jesus' distress.

1. With adults and teens:
    a. Encourage them to talk about how they are feeling. Sharing your own distresses might give them permission to talk about theirs.
    b. Or you might say, "If I were going through what you're experiencing, I would feel... (and share two or three distresses you might feel)." Then give them an opportunity to talk about their feelings.
    c. You might go over "What can I do *today* to lower my stress" with them, and work on each point together if they would like.

2. With children:

Children benefit tremendously when they are helped to identify and appropriately express their emotions. This can begin at a very early age. When they can *talk out* their feelings they are much less apt to *act them out*.

I (Ken) was counseling a couple whose three-year-old daughter was having severe temper tantrums. As we explored further, she seemed to have them when she would get frustrated. I asked the couple to give her a name for feelings, and kindly tell her she was frustrated each time. A week later they came back and said, "We can hardly believe the difference! The turning point came when she walked into the room and dropped her doll on the floor. We asked what was wrong and she replied, 'She's fwustwated!'"

A word of caution: As your child is learning this skill, be sure to avoid criticizing or belittling their feelings (even if you think there's no reason for them to feel that way). Respond with affirmation and empathy, and you'll be amazed at the results.

Chapter 7

Harness Your Resources
How can you enlist God's Help?

We have amazing resources for managing stress well.
- Many of these are "natural" resources, available to everyone, whether they know God or not. You'll learn more about these in Chapter 11.

- "Spiritual" resources are available only to those who follow the Lord. You'll discover more in Chapter 10.

Jesus gave us an example of how to use our natural and spiritual resources in managing stress. Even though Jesus was truly God, in His human condition He utilized natural and spiritual resources just as we must do when undergoing stress. A few of those resources were:

1. Prayer
2. The Word

3. His sonship with the Father

4. His relationships with others

5. Forgiveness

6. Joy

7. Knowing that He had fulfilled God's will

8. Trust in the Father

9. Rest

10. Sleep

11. The Holy Spirit

12. Spiritual warfare

We'll look at each of these, later in the chapter.

How Well Am I Using Spiritual Resources to Manage Stress?

Consider how well you are applying spiritual resources *when you are struggling with stress*, and use this scale to indicate your responses.

1 = Hardly ever, 2 = Occasionally,
3 = Sometimes, 4 = Often, 5 = Nearly always

_____ 1. I consciously choose to put my trust in God and in His working in my life. Psalm 56:3; Proverbs 3:5-6; Isaiah 12:2, 26:3-4; Nahum 1:7.

_____ 2. I am careful to confess sinful reactions, destructive attitudes, lack of faith, etc. Psalm 32:1-5; 1 John 1:9.

_____ 3. I ask God for what I need from Him to be able to handle the stress. 2 Samuel 22:7; Philippians 4:6-7; James 5:13.

_____ 4. I pour out my heart to God when I'm experiencing difficult stress. Psalm 55:22, 62:8; 1 Peter 5:7.

_____ 5. I choose to give thanks to God. 2 Corinthians 2:14;

Ephesians 5:20; Philippians 4:6-7.

_____ 6. I choose to worship Him in praise. Psalm 68:19; Hebrews 13:15.

_____ 7. I claim God's promises, especially those that bring comfort, strength, joy, and encouragement. Psalm 119:50, 52, 148, 162; Romans 4:20-21; 15:4.

_____ 8. I seek to apply the teachings of God's Word on how to cope with stress. Psalm 25:10, 119:100, 105; 2 Timothy 3:16-17.

_____ 9. I choose to rejoice in the Lord, even when the stress is difficult. Habakkuk 3:17-18; Philippians 4:4. (Paul spoke of joy fourteen times when he wrote to the Philippians from prison).

_____ 10. I take time to rest—in whatever ways I rest best. Matthew 11:28-30; Mark 6:31.

_____ 11. I sing and/or listen to music that helps lower my stress level. Psalm 32:7, 59:16-17, 77:6; Isaiah 12:2; Acts 16:25.

_____ 12. I share my burdens with others so they can help bear them. Numbers 11:10-17; Galatians 6:2.

_____ 13. I seek counsel and a biblical perspective from others. Colossians 3:16; 1 Thessalonians 5:14.

_____ 14. I allow others to comfort and encourage me. 2 Corinthians 1:3-4, 7:5-6; Hebrews 3:13, 10:24-25.

_____ 15. I ask others to pray for me. 2 Corinthians 1:11; Ephesians 6:18-20; James 5:16.

_____ 16. I rely on the Holy Spirit to guide and give me strength and wisdom. Mark 13:11; John 14:26; Romans 5:1-5.

_____ 17. I recognize when I am under attack from the enemy and I resist him. James 4:7; 1 Peter 5:6-9; Ephesians 6:10-18.

_____ 18. I share my burdens with God. Numbers 11:10-17.

Questions for personal or group study

1. Look up each of the following verses on Jesus' resources for stress. What can you learn from each?

   - Prayer (Matt. 26:36-44; John 17)

   - The Word (Luke 22:37)

   - His sonship with the Father (John 16:28, 17:1)

   - His relationships with others (Matt. 26:36-46; Luke 22:28)

   - Forgiveness (Luke 23:34)

   - Joy (John 15:11; Heb. 12:2)

   - Knowing that He had fulfilled God's will (John 17:4)

   - Trust in the Father (1 Pet. 2:23)

   - Rest (Mark 6:31-32; John 4:6)

   - Sleep (Luke 8:22-23)

   - The Holy Spirit (Luke 4:1-30)

   - Spiritual warfare (Matt. 16:21-23)

2. What spiritual resources are you already applying in your situation? List the ones you are using now, and how they are helping.

3. What spiritual resources have you not yet applied but would like to try? Specifically state how and when you will apply them.

What can I do *today* to lower my stress?

1. Look over your responses to "How Well am I Using Spiritual Resources to Manage Stress?" Prayerfully choose one or more resources you haven't been utilizing well, and write out what you will begin doing differently regarding them. Share with someone who will hold you accountable.

   a. Study the verses listed in the areas where you scored two or less. Ask the Lord what you need to do to improve in those areas. Then apply what He says.

   b. Which ones do you want to apply in your current stress situations?

2. Often we get stressed because we are trying to do everything in our own strength, rather than rely on the Holy Spirit. What do the following verses say to you?

Mark 13:11

John 14:26

Romans 8:26

Romans 15:13

3. Write at least one thing on the *Snapshots* pages (at the end of the book) that you want to remember and/or do. How can you apply it today?

How can I help others?

1. **For adults**, encourage them to take, "How Well Am I Using Spiritual Resources to Manage Stress?" Talk about what you both learned from it.

2. **With children or teens**, talk to them about what resources they have and can use. These are fabulous tools to give your children that they can use throughout their lives. The way you approach each of the resources will depend on the child's age. Don't discount their ability to understand. Even very young children can begin to pray and you can read the Word to them.

Chapter 8

Relieve the Pressure
How can you lower your stress?

Often just doing the first four skills is not enough. Sometimes you may need to take some other steps to relieve the stress.

The Word gives us many examples and teaching that we are to be active participants with God in doing something about our stressful situations.

One of the first questions to ask yourself is: "Can I get out of this stress situation?" If the answer is "yes" then consider, "Will God be pleased or displeased?" Your strategy will depend on the answer.

Here are three examples in The Word when the solution to stress was to get out of the situation.

1. When in prison, rather than passively accept his circumstances, Joseph did what he could to get out (Gen. 40:12-15).

2. When Paul went to Troas to preach the gospel, he had no peace of mind because he didn't find Titus there, so he left and went on to Macedonia (2 Cor. 2:12-13).

3. We can only imagine the pain Jesus felt when he heard that John the Baptist was beheaded. He dealt with it by withdrawing by boat privately to a solitary place (Matt. 14:13).

However, escape is often not a viable option. The consequences may be too great. You may be very stressed in a difficult job, but quitting could mean severe hardship for you and your family. Your new baby might cause more stress than you bargained for, but you aren't about to give her up for adoption!

In these situations we can apply the skills we're learning to reduce our stress reactions. One of our favorite and most effective strategies for handling stress is to ask another question, "Is this merely *junk stress*?"

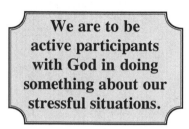

We are to be active participants with God in doing something about our stressful situations.

Junk stress is any stress in which the cost of keeping it is greater than the benefits and it is not sin to dump it. It can be external—in the situation, or internal—inside ourselves.

External junk stress may include such things as:
- activities
- commitments
- responsibilities

that cause stress but are not essential to your life.

When Bobbie and I (Ken) were new Bible translators in Guatemala, we thought it was our responsibility to meet *every* need we could of the Chuj people: care for all the sick no matter how far away they lived, vaccinate every child, teach everyone to read, pull every rotted tooth, and much more. We began to be worn out and the translation work suffered.

One day I hiked up a mountain to seek the Lord. He led me to write down all my responsibilities and how much time each took.

When I added it all up, it would take over 200 years to complete the New Testament! As good as these activities were, they were actually junk. That day God showed me the solution: train *them* to do it for themselves. The result was that the translation was completed in less than ten years, and the Chuj people were equipped to take care of most of their own needs.

Moses was a perfect example of dealing with external junk stress. Moses was working from morning to night, doing all the judging for the people. He thought he had to do it all. When his father-in-law Jethro saw this, instead of praising him for his hard work, he said, "What you are doing is not good. You and these people who come to you will only wear yourselves out. The work is too heavy for you; you cannot handle it alone" (Ex. 18:13-18). So Moses delegated the easy ones to others and only handled the difficult ones, and was "able to handle the strain."

Internal junk stress may include things like:
- fears when there is nothing to fear
- worries about the future
- false guilt
- unresolved anger that turns into resentment
- "what ifs" (see below)
- feeling rushed when there's no reason to be

Jesus spoke of junk stress when He said, "do not worry about tomorrow, for tomorrow will worry about itself" (Matt. 6:34).

Mark Twain beautifully illustrated internal junk stress when he said, "I have been through some terrible things in my life, some of which actually happened." As you look back on your life, how many of the terrible things you worried about didn't actually happen? It's easy to get so caught up in all the "what ifs" that we can become overwhelmed. *What if* my child gets run over by a bus? *What if* I lose my job? *What if...*?

Even Moses struggled with "what ifs," when he replied to God's call, "*What if* they do not believe me or listen to me...?"

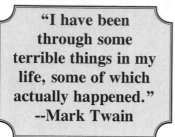

"I have been
through some
terrible things in my
life, some of which
actually happened."
--Mark Twain

(Ex. 4:1). In Exodus 3:13 Moses used a variation of "what if" when he said, "*Suppose* I go to the Israelites and say to them, 'The God of your fathers has sent me to you,' and they ask me, 'What is his name?' Then what shall I tell them?" (italics added).

What can I do *today* to lower my stress?

1. Look over your list of stressors again. As you do, try to identify at least one that you can get out of without serious consequences. Explore your options for how to escape. Then do it!

2. Go through your list of stress situations. Consider any that look like *external* junk stress. Then look at each one and think about what *internal* junk stress may be making the situation worse.

3. Choose one of your more difficult stressors, and identify how your *internal* junk stress may be making it worse. Begin by casting it on the Lord, and continue to do so every time it comes up. "Cast your cares on the Lord and He will sustain you" (Psa. 55:22).

   Note: It is very helpful to keep a written record of each junk stress you dump, so you can go back later and make sure it's gone.

4. Look over your list of stressors once more. Explore your options on how to do something about them. Talk over your ideas with your spouse or trusted friends, and ask for their counsel. Choose your options and begin working on them.

5. Write at least one thing on the *Snapshots* pages (at the end of the book) that you want to remember and/or do. How can you apply it today?

Questions for personal or group study

1. If in a group, share one stress situation, what you're doing about it, and how it's going.

2. Read Genesis 40:12-15 to discover what Joseph did about his stress.

3. Read the fascinating story in Exodus 18:13-27. How did Moses handle his junk stress?

4. How did Paul handle his stress in these situations?
   Corinthians 2:12-13

   1 Thessalonians 2:17-3:6

How can I help others?

As with any of the topics, you need to first work through it yourself, *before* you are able to help others.

1. With children:

    a. As soon as they can understand, begin using the term "stress" so they have a word to describe what they are experiencing.

    b. You may want to talk about one or two of your stressors (not the worst ones), how they affect you, and how you're handling them. This lets them know it's okay to talk about their stress.

    c. Help them explore their options for reducing or getting rid of each stress. I (Ken) have seen five-year-old children come up with very sensible, creative solutions to their stress by doing this. At that age they can also identify and dump their junk stress with some help.

    d. What can you do to help lower their stress? For example, are you pushing them to do too many things? Often parents have unrealistic expectations for their children, so they end up overwhelmed and discouraged.

2. With teens and adults:

    a. If they haven't already written up their list of stressors, encourage them to do that.

    b. Ask them if they would like to explore options with you to discover how they can lower their stress levels. If you do this, it's better—for the most part—if you just ask them questions. Let them think through what might work for them.

    c. Talk about or read the section on junk stress. Have them look at what kinds of junk stress might be affecting them.

Chapter 9

Transform Your Circumstances

How will focusing on God help you?

This skill is the last, even though it is the most important of all six. We've put it last because often people want to "spiritualize" stress and then they fail to work through the process of managing it. God has given us all of the skills for managing stress that we've talked about—not just this one.

Focusing on God and eternal realities can transform the most difficult and stressful circumstances into experiences of joy and God's blessing.

In the *Door to Joy,** I (Gaylyn) share about how God transformed my circumstances and surprised me with amazing joy when I was in the middle of one of the most difficult times of my life. My second son, Daniel, was born with multiple problems with his brain, heart and lungs. (This is a great simplification.) During my son's first three months, I focused on how terrible things were, how overwhelming. And guess what? I got more and more overwhelmed and depressed. The situation looked impossible.

I doubt anyone will dispute the fact that my stress situation was huge. But I made it even bigger because of my internal stress, which distorted my perception and therefore my total stress.

During Daniel's first three months, my perception was that everything was terrible. Horrible. Unfair. During Daniel's next three months, I set aside my internal stress and began to focus on God, rather than my problems. I saw that God is bigger and more powerful than any disease. Guess what? Things didn't seem nearly as bad or as overwhelming.

Was Daniel better those next three months? No. Actually, he was worse. I found out my son had less than a year to live. My son was dying, but I was not as overwhelmed, discouraged or depressed as I had been. In fact, I had an amazing peace and joy—like I'd never had before. Why? Because I chose to focus on God rather than on my circumstances. That's the only thing that changed in my life. I chose to see how good and powerful He is, recognizing that nothing is too hard for Him. The change in my perception of my situation—though not always easy to maintain—gave me strength and courage to face each day.

> **Focusing on God can transform the most difficult and stressful circumstances into experiences of joy and God's blessing.**

Then one day, God completely healed my son! Well ... that was my perspective as I held Daniel's lifeless body in my arms. I knew that he was with Jesus—completely healed and perfect. He would never suffer again. Was it the kind of healing I prayed for? No. But through my tears, my first thought after he died was that he was healed. Tears mingled with joy. I would miss him, yet I knew I would see him again.

When I focus on the Lord, my problems seem to shrink in comparison with God's greatness and power.

Your perspective can make all the difference between feeling overwhelmed by trouble or being surprised by joy. And it can change the little, annoying stressors of life into opportunities to worship God rather than merely feeling irritated and grumpy.

In the *Door to Joy* I (Ken) recalled arriving at the Islamabad (Pakistan) airport, eager to fly home after three stressful weeks of counseling. When I got up to the counter, I was told they didn't have my reservation and there was no chance of getting on the flight. Stressed? I sure was. I had almost no money, no contacts in the area and nowhere to go. I made a difficult choice: I sat down in the airport and begin thanking and praising God for everything I could think of. Thirty minutes later I heard my name called, and miraculously got on the flight! But the greater miracle was that God had transformed my stress into true joy and complete peace.

Perhaps the Apostle Paul put it best when the Holy Spirit inspired him to write:

Therefore we do not lose heart.
Though outwardly we are wasting away,
yet inwardly we are being renewed day by day.
For our light and momentary troubles
are achieving for us an eternal glory
that far outweighs them all.
So we fix our eyes not on what is seen, but on what is unseen.
For what is seen is temporary,
but what is unseen is eternal.
2 Corinthians 4:16-18

Paul had an amazing perspective. It seems like he must have had an easy life, because He talks about "our light and momentary troubles." That's definitely not true. If you read 2 Corinthians 11:23-29 you'll discover some of the stresses he experienced: he was flogged severely, exposed to death, beaten with rods and whips, stoned and shipwrecked. He was in danger from rivers, bandits and his own countrymen. He was cold, naked, hungry, and much more. Read it for yourself.

How could Paul handle all the pressure? By focusing on what is unseen—the Lord and heaven.

Once more, Jesus is our example. Throughout the gospels we find He consistently set His mind and heart on His Father, and spoke of the deep spiritual reality embedded in the situation. This brought Him great joy, even in suffering. Luke 10:21 says, "At that time Jesus, full of joy through the Holy Spirit, said, "I praise you, Father, Lord of heaven and earth, because you have hidden these things from the wise and learned, and revealed them to little children. Yes, Father, for this was your good pleasure."

We can learn so much about managing our difficult stress situations effectively as we "fix our eyes on Jesus" and "consider Him who endured... so that we will not grow weary and lose heart," (Heb. 12:2-3).

Many other verses emphasize this skill. You are encouraged to discover them for yourselves. One of our favorites is found in 2 Chronicles 20. A "vast army" was coming to destroy the little nation of Judah. The situation seemed hopeless, but their leader, Jehoshaphat, engaged in some seemingly very strange (but effective) strategies to deal with it. One of them is found in verse 12. He talked to God about how hopeless their situation looked. Then he said, "We do not know what to do, *but our eyes are* upon *you."* You'll get a chance to study this fascinating chapter under *Questions for Personal or Group Study*.

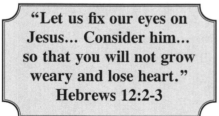

"Let us fix our eyes on Jesus... Consider him... so that you will not grow weary and lose heart."
Hebrews 12:2-3

Over the years we've both had a passion to know God better. I (Gaylyn) started meditating daily on God's names and qualities when my son was dying. Over the years I have compiled a list of over 1300 names of God. I never in my wildest imagination thought there would be that many names. I started a blog to help others focus on who God is. You can check it out: www. DailyNameofGod.com.

Questions for personal or group study

1. How has focusing on the Lord and eternal realities helped you?

2. Read 2 Chronicles 20:1-26 for one of the most amazing stories in the entire Bible, with powerful principles on how to handle incredibly difficult circumstances.

   a. What "distress" did Jehoshaphat have? What distresses would you have had in that situation? Go back to chapter 6 if you need to be reminded about distresses.

   b. Study Jehoshaphat's prayer in verses 3-12. In what ways is his prayer like yours when you are in a crisis? How are you challenged to pray differently?

   c. Consider how praying as he did would lower your stress level.

   d. How did the people go out to face their enemies (verses 21-22)? Think about what they were doing, considering they were going out to face a huge army.

      Verse 22 is one of my (Gaylyn's) favorite verses in the Bible. It says, "*As they began* to sing and praise, the LORD set ambushes against the men ... who were invading Judah, and they were defeated" (italics added). Notice *when* the Lord chose to defeat their enemy. Keep reading for the rest of the story!

e. What will you apply from this chapter to your life?

3. Read the following passages. What can you learn from them? Write down, or discuss your thoughts.

2 Corinthians 4:16-18

Hebrews 12:2-3

Colossians 3:1-2

4. What do you do now to focus on God and eternal realities? Write down what others share. You may find insights from others that will help you.

What can I do *today* to lower my stress?

1. Reflect on and write down: "What am I doing now to keep my focus on God, and on eternal realities?"

2. Consider: "How can I focus on the Lord more, or better? Alone? With others?"

3. Write at least one thing on the *Snapshots* pages (at the end of the book) that you want to remember and/or do. How can you apply it today?

How can I help others?

1. For adults and teens:
   - Share how focusing on God has helped you.

   - Talk about some of the verses in this chapter.

   - Ask them how thinking about eternity and the Lord has helped them in the past and how it encourages them now.

2. With children:
   - Daily spend time talking to them about how great God is. It's never too early for them to get to know the Lord.

   - Teach them about heaven and stir up in them an excitement about going there. When my oldest son Jonathan was three, we often talked about heaven and sang, "Heaven is a wonderful place, filled with glory and grace. I want to see my Savior's face. Heaven is a wonderful place. I wanna go there." When his six-month old brother Daniel died, holding him Jonathan said, "Let's sing, 'Heaven is a wonderful place.'" He knew where his brother was!

> "Heaven is a wonderful place, filled with glory and grace. I want to see my Savior's face. Heaven is a wonderful place. I wanna go there."

---

* For more information on the *Door to Joy* or to get a copy of it, go to www. RelationshipResources.org

Part Three
Maximize Your Resources

As God's children we have immeasurable resources at our disposal for managing stress effectively. God provides these resources so we can live abundant, fruitful lives even under great amounts of stress. They are our *greatest source* of help in times of stress.

Paul's prayer in Colossians 1:9-14 illustrates some of these resources. However, applying spiritual resources does *not* automatically keep us from experiencing distress.

Jesus experienced *profound* distress as he went to the cross. See chapter 6. Let's not fall into the trap of thinking that our spiritual resources aren't working because we *feel bad*.

Chapter 10

Empower Your Potential
How can the Bible help you?

We have incredible treasures waiting for us to uncover. Each one is found in the Word. We encourage you to make a habit to spend time in the Word discovering all God has for you. In this chapter we will look very briefly at some of our key spiritual resources.

Spiritual resources are *objective* and *subjective* in nature. Objective resources exist independently of us. Their power is without limit, but we must grasp them by employing our subjective resources, through our knowledge of God.

Make your own ongoing study of God's Word, and discover for yourself resources you can use most effectively as you face stressful situations.

Objective Resources

Our objective resources come from who God is and what He does. Each of these resources can be seen from three viewpoints:

a. *Identity:* Who He is

b. *Attributes:* What He is like

c. *Functions:* What He does for us

There are many more verses that illustrate each point. Here are a few examples to give you ideas for further study. You will be wonderfully blessed and helped if you begin studying through the Word to discover more about His incredible resources, not just for managing stress, but for living the abundant life that Jesus promised us in John 10:10.

1. God the Father.

a. *Identity*: He is the Father of compassion and God of all comfort (2 Cor. 1:3).

b. *Attributes*: He is compassionate, gracious, slow to anger, abounding in love (Psa. 103:8).

c. *Functions*: He comforts us in our troubles (2 Cor. 1:4).

Past: He anointed us (2 Cor. 1:21), set His seal of ownership on us (2 Cor. 1:22), put His Spirit in our hearts (2 Cor. 1:22, 5:5), made His light shine in our hearts (2 Cor. 4:6), and reconciled us to Himself (2 Cor. 5:18).

Present: He comforts us (2 Cor. 1:4, 7:6-7), makes us stand firm (2 Cor. 1:21), always leads us in triumphal procession (2 Cor. 2:14), makes us competent (2 Cor. 3:5-6), renews us inwardly daily (2 Cor. 4:16), lives and walks among us (2 Cor. 6:16).

Future: He will deliver us (2 Cor. 1:10), will raise us and present us in His presence (2 Cor. 4:14), and will give us an eternal body (2 Cor. 5:1).

2. God the Son.

   a. *Identity:* He is the Shepherd and Overseer of our souls (1 Pet. 2:25).

   b. *Attributes:* He is faithful (Heb. 3:6) and gentle (Matt. 11:29).

   c. *Functions:*

      Past: He died for us and was raised again (Rom. 8:34), became poor for our sakes (2 Cor. 8:9).

      Present: He gives us rest (Matt. 11:28), He sympathizes with our weaknesses (Heb. 4:15), He lives in us (2 Cor. 13:5), The promises of God are YES in Him (2 Cor. 1:19-20), His power rests on us as we look to Him in weakness (2 Cor: 12:9).

      Future: He will come again and take us to Himself (John 14:3), destroy him who has the power of death (Heb. 2:14) and do whatever we ask in His name (John 14:13-14).

3. God the Holy Spirit.

   a. *Identity:* He is our Counselor or Comforter (John 14:26).

   b. *Attributes:* He is the Truth (John 14:17) and the Life (Rom. 8:2).

   c. *Functions:* He helps us in our weakness and intercedes for us (Rom. 8:26), teach us (John 14:16), guides us into all truth (John 16:13).

4. God's Word.

   a. *Identity:* It is the sword of the Spirit (Eph. 6:17).

   b. *Attributes:* It is living and active, sharper than any double-edged sword (Heb. 4:12).

   c. *Functions:* It gives endurance and encouragement (Rom.15:4).

God's word does more than 50 wonderful things for us! See

how many you can discover. You can start with 2 Timothy 3:16-17: "All Scripture is God-breathed and is useful for teaching, rebuking, correcting and training in righteousness, so that the man of God may be thoroughly equipped for every good work."

4. **The Body of Christ.** Other believers are a powerful resource in stressful times. Many verses emphasize this. In Colossians 2:2, Paul prayed that believers' "hearts may be encouraged as they are knit together in love" (RSV). Are you *knit together* with others in love? God never intended that we try to handle life's struggles alone. Here are just a few ways we help each other in times of stress.

   a. Prayer (2 Cor. 1:11; Eph. 6:18-20; James 5:16)

   b. Mutual upbuilding (Rom. 14:19; 1 Thess. 5:11)

   c. Mutual comfort (2 Cor. 1:3-4, 7:5-6)

   d. Mutual encouragement (Heb. 3:13, 10:24-25)

   e. Mutual burden bearing (Gal. 6:2)

   f. Counsel, etc. (Col. 3:16; 1 Thess. 5:14)

The Bridge of Knowledge

1. Before objective resources can be useful to us we must cross the *bridge of knowledge*.

2. We must come to know God and His Word, not only intellectually, but experientially, on a *heart level*.

   "His divine power has given us everything we need for life and godliness through our knowledge of him..." (2 Pet. 1:3). Our heart knowledge of God enables us to draw on Him during times of stress, and so utilize our subjective resources.

Subjective Resources

Our subjective resources come from within us and others in the body of Christ. God doesn't want us to merely expect Him to do everything for us. We must also take the initiative to be actively involved in the process.

1. **Faith.** We need faith to integrate and take advantage of all of God's resources. Hebrews 11:1 describes two types of faith.

    a. **"Assurance"** (Greek: *hupostasis*) is passive, resting faith. It literally means a foundation, the ground on which one builds a hope. It is a defensive weapon (Eph. 6:16).

    b. **"Conviction"** (Greek: *elegchos*) is active, assertive faith. It means proving or testing, a proving of unseen things. Most of the heroes in Hebrews 11 demonstrated assertive faith.

    c. Together active and passive faith form one powerful resource for handling stress.

2. **Spiritual Vision.**

    a. In a time of extreme stress, Moses "persevered because he saw Him who is invisible" (Heb. 11:12).

    b. Ephesians 1:15-19 asks God to enlighten the eyes of our hearts so we may be able to see the unseen spiritual reality of God's objective resources.

    c. In 2 Corinthians 4:18, Paul spoke of fixing his eyes on what is unseen rather than on what is seen.

    d. This is a growth process in which we must be actively involved. The ability to see beyond our physical situation and perceive spiritual reality enables us to take advantage of God's powerful resources for handling stress well.

    > It's revealing to take a good look at ourselves in the light of the Word. But then we must turn our minds from ourselves to Jesus.

3. **Prayer.** Prayer brings us into direct, immediate contact with the Lord. Faith and spiritual vision are necessary for effective prayer. All three are essential for managing stress. These five types of prayer help us in stress situations. You might add others.

   a. Confession of sinful reactions (Psa. 32:1-5; 1 John 1:9)

   b. Petition for God's help (Phil. 4:6-7)

   c. Pouring out our hearts to God (Psa. 55:22, 62:8)

   d. Thanksgiving (2 Cor. 2:14; Eph. 5:20; Phil. 4:6-7)

   e. Praise (Psa. 68:19; Heb. 13:15)

> **Our heart knowledge of God enables us to draw on Him during times of stress.**

4. **Knowledge.** "We have the light of the knowledge of the glory of God in the face of Christ" (2 Cor. 4:6). "We *know* [are convinced of, fully confident] that He will also raise us with Jesus" (2 Cor. 4:14). "Now we *know* that if the earthly tent we live in is destroyed, we have a building from God, an eternal house in heaven" (2 Cor. 5:1, italics added). As we gain more and more knowledge of God and His promises, and as we consider these truths, we grow in our stamina during stressful times.

5. **Affirmation of who we are in Christ**. We know that we are:

   a. The temple of the living God (2 Cor. 6:16)

   b. His people (2 Cor. 6:16)

   c. Sent by God (2 Cor. 2:17)

   d. His children (2 Cor. 6:18)

   e. Christ's ambassadors (2 Cor. 5:20)

6. **Spiritual Warfare.** The enemy comes to steal, kill and destroy us (John 10:10). We need to be so in tune with our Shepherd's

voice that we can instantly recognize when He is not the one speaking to us. (John 10:1-5). The following are some ways to do warfare against Satan and his forces:

a. *Put on our armor* (Eph. 6:10-18). Just as we would never think about going out without our clothes, we need to get into the habit of putting on our armor every day to protect us from an attack from the enemy.

b. *Remind Satan of his defeat* by claiming Jesus' blood. Revelation 12:11 says, "They overcame him by the blood of the Lamb."

c. *Binding and loosing*. (Mat 18:18) Bind demonic forces. Loose the angels of the Lord and the Spirit of the Living God.

d. *Praise*. Praise and worship remind us and the enemy that God is bigger than he is and nothing is impossible for the Lord. Just praising God can route the enemy as we see in 2 Chronicles 20:22: "As they began to sing and praise, the LORD set ambushes against ... and they were defeated." (See all of 2 Chron. 20).

e. *Pray with authority*. Ephesians 2:6 says we are "seated with Him in the heavenly realms in Christ Jesus." We can pray from a place of authority, because we are seated with the King of Kings in the heavenly realms. From that position, Satan has no power or authority.

7. **Other Subjective Resources:**

a. Joy (Neh. 8:10)

b. Rest (Matt. 11:28-30)

c. Peace (John 14:27)

d. Accept weaknesses and be content with them under stress (2 Cor. 11:29-30, 12:5-10)

e. Set our hope on Him (2 Cor. 1:10)

f. Refuse to lose heart or get discouraged

(2 Cor. 4:1, 16)

g. Choose to be confident in Him (2 Cor. 5:6, 8)

h. Make it our goal (consuming ambition) to please Him (2 Cor. 5:9)

i. Our purity and patience (2 Cor. 6:6)

j. Choose to rejoice, even in affliction (2 Cor. 6:10, 8:2, 12:10)

k. Refuse to compare ourselves with others (2 Cor. 10:12)

We trust you will continue to study each of these areas. We have just barely revealed the tip of the iceberg on each one.

Note: The Appendix has additional biblical resources.

Healing In 2 Corinthians

Paul's second letter to the Corinthian church provides many insights into how to endure in difficult circumstances. He talked about at least 45 kinds of stress he had experienced. Healsosharedmany of the spiritual resources he found effective in enabling him to cope with those difficult situations.

In this letter, God gives us at least ten principles for healing the pain caused by hurtful stress in our lives, based on Paul's life. He experienced many wounds, and the Holy Spirit revealed these principles for our benefit.

Study these passages carefully, and begin applying them to any pain you have. (See the discussion in Chapter 3 on "Sore Spots".)

1. Acknowledge the pain (1:8-10, 2:4)

2. Share the pain with God (12:8)

3. Share it with others (1:8-9, 6:4)

4. Ask others for prayer (1:11)

5. Allow God to heal through His comfort, directly or through others (1:3-4)

6. Repent if you're aware of any sin in your life (7:9-10)

7. Forgive if others caused your pain (2:7-11)

8. Fix your eyes on the Lord and on eternal realities (2:14, 4:18)

9. Accept God's grace in place of your weakness (12:9-10)

10. Give thanks to God, especially in times of pain (2:14)

Psalm 31
An Example of Handling Stress

In Psalm 31, God provides a helpful example from David's life on how to utilize His resources for handling stress in extreme circumstances. Study this Psalm for creative ways to handle your own stress.

The Intensity of David's Stress

Verses 9-13 indicate the intensity of the stress David was experiencing, and the resulting symptoms. He experienced severe symptoms in the following areas:

- emotional (9, 10)
- physical (10)
- social and interpersonal (11)
- mental (12)

Nearly every aspect of his life was severely affected by stress.

David's Strategy for Handling the Stress

David demonstrated several specific behaviors and attitudes in his strategy for handling this intensely difficult situation. His primary method for dealing with it centered around his intimate relationship with God, as indicated by his first statement, "In you, O Lord, I have taken refuge" (Ps. 31:1). Let's look at how He handled the stress by taking refuge in the Lord.

In this Psalm, the Holy Spirit gives us fourteen specific things to do in our relationship with our Lord when in a stressful situation.

    a. Use this study as a checklist to make sure you're employing as many of God's resources as possible.

    b. Then you may want to study other passages in the Word and add other specific skills to your strategy.

1. He set his heart and mind on who God is.

    a. My rock and my fortress (3)

    b. My refuge (4)

    c. Lord, the God of truth (5)

    d. You are my God (14)

2. He set his heart and mind on God's attributes.

    a. His righteousness (1)

    b. His truth (5)

    c. His wonderful, unfailing love (7, 16, 21)

    d. His great goodness (19)

3. He cried to God for help (1, 17).

4. He committed his spirit to God (5).

5. He affirmed his trust in the Lord (6, 14).

6. He reminded himself of what God had done (5, 7, 8, 19, 21, 22).

7. He chose to be glad and rejoice (7).

8. He acknowledged his pain and suffering, and described it to God (9-13).

9. He reminded himself that his times were in God's hands (15).

10. He praised the Lord (21).

11. He reminded himself of what God does for His own children (20, 23).

12. He expressed what He wanted God to be to him.

    a. Be my rock of refuge, a strong fortress to save me (2).

b. Be merciful to me (9).

13. He prayed for what He wanted God to do for him.

a. Let me never be put to shame (1)

b. Deliver me (1, 15)

c. Turn your ear to me (2)

d. Come quickly to my rescue (2)

e. Lead and guide me (3)

f. Free me from the trap (4)

g. Let your face shine on me (16)

h. Save me in your unfailing love (16)

i. Let me not be put to shame (17)

> David's primary method for dealing with stress centered around his intimate relationship with God.

14. In the middle of his stress, He encouraged others.

a. To love the Lord (23)

b. To be strong and take heart (24)

We pray that you will increase your skills for handling stress as you study David's strategy.

What can I do *today* to lower my stress?

1. Choose one of the "Objective Resources" to begin applying today, from the beginning of this chapter. For example, "When I feel stressed I will stop and consider God's faithfulness to me all these years."

2. Choose one of the "Subjective Resources" to apply this week. For example, "In the midst of my stress I will choose to praise and thank God for everything I can think of."

3. Write at least one thing on the *Snapshots* pages (at the end of the book) that you want to remember and/or do. How can you apply it today?

Questions for personal or group study

Here are several Bible studies based on the material on stress. Look them over, and choose which ones would be most helpful in your life right now.

1. Study each of the verses listed in "Healing in 2 Corinthians" in this chapter.

   a. Which, if any, of these principles have you not considered in terms of bringing healing for your internal stress?

   b. Which principles do you want to make more a part of your life?

2. Study the verses listed in Psalm 31: "An Example of Handling Stress."

    a. Which of David's strategies are you using now?

    b. In which do you want to grow?

3. Study the verses that describe our objective resources.

    a. Which of these do you choose to focus on when you are under stress?

    b. Which ones do you want to focus on more?

    c. How can you make them more real to you?

4. Then consider the verses that describe our subjective resources.

    a. Which of these do you consciously turn to when you're under stress?

    b. Which ones do you want to begin using more?

    c. How can you use them better?

How can I help others?

1. For adults: Suggest doing any, or all, of the studies together under "Questions for personal or group study."

2. For children:

    a. Talk with them about who God is and what He does for them (Objective Resources). When my (Ken) 4-year-old great-granddaughter was afraid to go into the dark basement, her mother talked about how God is always with her. Soon after she went downstairs on her own. When her mother asked her why she wasn't afraid, she said, "I'm not afraid anymore. I take God with me."

    b. Read Psalm 31 with them, in an easy-to-understand translation. Talk about what helped David when He was having problems.

    c. Share with them, on their level, times when you were struggling and found God's help: what you did, how you did it, and how God worked.

Chapter 11

Uncover Treasure
What other resources are available?

In the last chapter, we looked at *spiritual resources* to handle the normal and extraordinary stresses of life. These are our first line of defense in dealing with stress. However, God has also given us common sense to use in dealing with life.

Ephesians 5:15 says, "Be very careful, then, how you live—not as unwise, but as wise." Practical resources are, in fact, spiritual, but we do not often think of them that way.

When you look at these resources, remember that God created each of us differently. What *reduces* stress for one person may *increase* stress for someone else. For example, shopping lowers stress for some people, but it increases mine (Gaylyn). We need to learn to accept each other the way we are.

Here are some practical resources which will help you live with the stress of life in a wise way. When we employ these, we are using the common sense God has given us to live in healthy ways.

1. **Sleep**. We can miss sleep on occasion and function on less sleep for periods of time. But prolonged periods of inadequate sleep will significantly reduce our ability to cope with the normal stresses of life, let alone extraordinary stress that may happen. Answer the following questions:

   a. Do you know how much sleep you need to function at your best? Are you getting that much on a regular basis? If not, what do you need to do?

   b. Do you have a consistent pattern of sleep—a regular time to go to bed and a regular time to rise?

   c. Do you go to bed at a reasonable time or do you often stay up working, reading or watching TV?

   d. Do you have trouble getting to sleep or staying asleep? If so, have you tried to figure out why or what you may need to do to sleep more or better?

   e. What might you need to change to get more or better sleep?

> **When we employ practical resources to manage stress, we are using the sound mind God has given us to live in healthy ways.**

2. **Diet.** "You are what you eat" may be truer than we think. A healthy diet leads to a healthy body which increases your capacity to handle stress. A recent survey, by the American Psychological Association, found that almost half of adults say they eat too much or unhealthy foods when stressed and many people skip meals when under stress.

   a. What you eat affects your capacity to handle stress. Coffee, chocolate, tea, colas, and other foods high in caffeine pump adrenaline into your system and increase your stress. Sweets can have a similar effect on your system.

      These may not affect all people the same. However, it is important to consider a healthy well-balanced diet where these elements are taken in moderation.

      Ask yourself: Do I use caffeine or sugar to keep me going when I should be resting or sleeping?

   b. How much you eat also affects your capacity to handle stress. This is most true in terms of your weight.

      • Do you know your optimum weight for your height? Are you too short for your weight?

      • Excess weight, even if you are not considered obese, increases the stress on your body and decreases the energy available for handling normal stresses.

      • It is also possible to be underweight because you are too busy to eat or are preoccupied with looking good. Neither extreme is healthy.

3. **Physical Exercise.** It does not have to be physically exhausting. Brisk walking for thirty minutes a day can do wonders in managing stress. One study revealed that students who walked and did other easy-to-moderate exercise regularly had lower stress levels than couch potatoes or those who exercised strenuously.

   a. Regular physical exercise strengthens the heart and lungs which increases and maintains the body's ability to deal with the physiological effects of stress.

b. It also increases the blood flow to the brain which improves concentration and decision-making ability.

c. Exercise generates endorphins which improve perspective.

d. All three of these factors improve your ability to deal with stress. They have an impact even on your ability to use spiritual resources.

The key to exercise is being consistent.

4. **Physical Relaxation.** Several physical relaxation techniques can help you in times of severe stress or can help high-strung people deal with life in general. These would include:

a. breathing from the diaphragm

b. Tense-and-relax muscle exercises

c. a hot bath

d. a short nap

e. A massage

5. **Lifestyle.** Some stress is the result of our lives not being in order.

a. This relates to the idea of "junk stress." See chapter 3.

b. Try to identify areas of your life that are out of balance and which may be causing unnecessary stress.

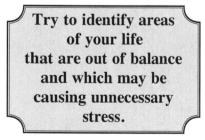

Try to identify areas of your life that are out of balance and which may be causing unnecessary stress.

6. **Mental Relaxation.** Mental relaxation could include:

a. listening to soothing music while lying down or reclining

b. reading a favorite novel

c. watching a good movie

d. playing games, if they are relaxing for you—for example, video games are relaxing for my (Gaylyn) sons, but are very stressful for me.

e. going for a walk to a peaceful or beautiful spot

f. laughter through reading, videos, jokes, etc.

7. **Relationships.** Being loved, valued, and cared for in our relationships is a shelter from stress. Just as loving parents calm an injured child with their love, so good relationships can be a healing balm. For this reason we need at least one supportive relationship in our lives—a relationship in which we can talk about anything that may be stressing us. See 2 Timothy 1:16-18.

We also need to work out conflicts in the important relationships in our lives such as spouses, children, supervisors, co-workers, neighbors, and friends. We need to resolve hurt and anger quickly, "so that the devil will not gain a foothold" (Eph. 4:26-27).

> We need to resolve hurt and anger quickly, "so that the devil will not gain a foothold."

An important part of good relationships is taking time to have fun together. It's easy to let work crowd out fun in our lives. Take time to:

a. have dinner or dessert with friends

b. go for a picnic

c. have a party or play games

d. do anything that you enjoy together

8. **Day of Rest.** Many believers think relaxing is the same as being slothful or lazy. They think the more they work and the busier they are, the more spiritual they are. Yet, often the Lord reminds us to rest. One of our favorite commands of Jesus to His disciples was, "Come with me by yourselves to a quiet place and get some rest." (Mark 6:31).

God even modeled the principle for us in Genesis 2:2 when "on the seventh day *he rested from all his work*" (italics added).

Before my son Timothy and I (Gaylyn) went to Israel, I

always thought the Sabbath was a legalistic day that was just part of the Old Testament law. When we were in Israel, I found out it's actually a day of great joy. The Jews eagerly anticipate it as a precious gift from God—a time to set aside concerns, relax, have fun, and enjoy relationships with God and family.

In Mark 2:27, Jesus said, "The Sabbath was made for man, not man for the Sabbath." God knows we can be more effective in our lives and work if we take the time to slow down and change our pace—especially in today's fast-paced, overworked world.

We want to encourage you to get into the habit of setting aside one day a week to take it easy—not because you have to or you'll be judged, but because you'll be blessed!

9. **Other Ideas.** The following are a few other possible resources to manage stress. The reason we say possible is that for some people, these ideas will reduce stress, for others, they will increase stress. We need to each figure out what helps us lower our stress level and what raises it.

    a. Shopping

    b. Pets or other animals. Someone recently told me (Gaylyn) that his farm animals are a great stress reducer. I can't imagine a cow or a chicken helping to reduce my stress, but ... we're each different

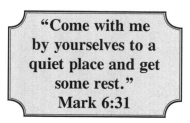

"Come with me by yourselves to a quiet place and get some rest."
Mark 6:31

    c. Watching or playing sports

    d. Name your own

This section is adapted from an article by Steven G. Edlin MA LCPC MFT

Questions for personal or group study

1. Ephesians 5:15 says, "Be very careful, then, how you live—not as unwise but as wise." What does it mean to you? What one change can you make to live more wisely?

2. Which resources help you the most? Why?

3. Which resources are the most difficult for you to apply? How could others help you apply them to your life?

4. Look at the following verses. What is the Lord saying to you through each?

   - Psalm 62:5: "Find rest, O my soul, in God alone; my hope comes from him."

   - Psalm 91:1: "He who dwells in the shelter of the Most High will rest in the shadow of the Almighty."

   - Psalm 116: "Be at rest once more, O my soul, for the LORD has been good to you."

5. Matthew 11:28-29 says, "Come to me, all you who are weary and burdened, and I will give you rest. Take my yoke upon you and learn from me, for I am gentle and humble in heart, and you will find rest for your souls." We need rest for our souls (our hearts and minds), as well as for our bodies.

   a. Remember a time you felt weary and burdened and the Lord gave you rest.

   b. What is the Lord saying to you today through these verses?

   c. In what ways have you experienced Jesus' rest?

6. Consider Thessalonians 4:11: "Make it your ambition to lead a quiet life, to mind your own business and to work with your hands, just as we told you." (Note: The Greek word for "quiet life" means tranquility of life, the idea of controlled quietness.) What can you learn and apply to your life today from this verse?

What can I do *today* to lower my stress?

1. Choose one of the resources in this chapter that could help you reduce your stress. What will you begin doing today to use it?

2. Take some time off today, or decide on a day this week you will take time to relax and recharge. When will you do it?

3. Write at least one thing on the *Snapshots* pages (at the end of the book) that you want to remember and/or do. How can you apply it today?

How can I help others?

1. For adults:
   a. Talk about any of the areas mentioned in this chapter that are difficult for you. Often, sharing our personal struggles will encourage others to share more deeply.

   b. Pray for each other.

   c. You might want to be accountable to each other in any specific areas that are hard for you.

2. For children:

    a. Are you helping them to eat right and get enough sleep and exercise? If not, what might you need to change?

    b. Are you being a good example to them in each area mentioned in this chapter? Children will do what you do much more than they will do what you say. What might you need to change?

    c. Consider having a family day of rest each week. Make it a day that the children anticipate.

Chapter 12

Discover Amazing Secrets
What are some additional strategies?

The apostle Paul was an incredible person, but not without his problems. Amazingly, he endured many difficulties and hardships, as well as struggling with many weaknesses.

To discover Paul's secret of emotional health under stress, join me (Ken) in an imaginary journey back in time, to interview him. Paul was in Rome under guard. He happily consented to the interview.*

As you read through this, think about:
    a. What were some of Paul's key strategies for managing stress?

b. Which of his strategies do you want to apply more in your own life?

K: (Ken) Paul, I've studied your letters and Luke's vivid description of your long and fruitful life of service. You are truly amazing!

P: (Paul) Why would you say that? I really haven't done anything out of the ordinary.

K: Well, you talked a lot about your weaknesses and struggles. Yet you traveled all over the world as you knew it and shared the Gospel everywhere. You endured really hard stuff that would have blown me away. But you made it, and you seem to be really healthy emotionally.

P: If you've read my letters, then you know that I did it in Christ's strength, not my own. That's the key. Remember? His power is made perfect in my weakness. Living in His strength rather than my own made the difference for me.

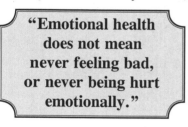

"**Emotional health does not mean never feeling bad, or never being hurt emotionally.**"

K: Yeah, but there's got to be more to it than that. In your second letter to the Corinthian Christians, you talked about forty-five different kinds of terrible hardships you had experienced; but you came through all of them well! Come on; tell me how you did it.

P: You counted all those struggles? I didn't realize I had gone on about them so much. Okay, I'll let you in on a few of my strategies, but you'll have to dig the rest of them out of the Word.

The first thing that comes to mind is that I'm very free to feel and express my emotions. I like to call it being "HOT"— honest, open and transparent. I don't apologize or feel guilty about my feelings, and I freely share them with my friends. Being honest with myself, God and others about my feelings is one of my secrets to emotional health.

K: Wow! That's awesome. Most of us modern people are slow to talk about our feelings, especially our painful ones. We're so reluctant that sometimes we even try to tell ourselves we don't feel them. We're afraid we won't be seen as spiritual, I guess.

As you can tell, I like to count things. I counted no less than thirty-three different feelings you mentioned in your letters, and twenty of those were what we call negative—feelings like

- fear

- anxiety

- shame

- regret

- anguish

- humiliation

- and a lot more

P: Of course it is. You twenty-first century people must be really messed up! Don't you see how we Bible characters are so HOT about our feelings? This is being just like God. Doesn't He feel all kinds of feelings and talk about them? Why can't we? In fact, when we do, we take the first step to emotional health.

You can't lie about how you feel and be healthy, whether you're talking about physical or emotional health. So tell your friends to be honest and not be ashamed of their

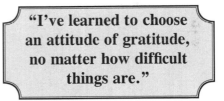

> "I've learned to choose an attitude of gratitude, no matter how difficult things are."

feelings. Tell them to encourage each other to be honest, and don't condemn each other for what they feel.

By the way, they need to know that emotional health does *not* mean never feeling bad, or never being hurt emotionally. Remember, physical health doesn't mean we're never sick or wounded, but that we bounce back to health again. In the same way, emotionally healthy people can be wounded, but they bounce back.

K: That's really helpful, Paul. What else has helped you keep healthy emotionally all these years?

P: Well, I've had a lot of help from others. In fact, I couldn't survive without them. I went out of my way to build strong relationships with friends and co-workers. They have ministered to me, not only in practical ways but to my emotional needs too. And I've also ministered to them.

> **"Did you know we have a choice to rejoice, no matter what the circumstances?"**

God never intended for us to serve Him alone, without others alongside us. I'll never forget how often Onesiphorus refreshed me when I was in prison in Ephesus. And how God comforted and strengthened me through friends like Timothy, Titus, Phoebe, Silas and even Mark. I wonder how many people God used to help me through hard times.

K: I counted seventy-seven people that you mentioned in your letters.

P: You really do like to count things, don't you? I've heard that some of you modern people try to get along without much help from others.

K: When I became a missionary like you, most organizations seemed to want independent people who could make it on their own. We all thought that needing others was a weakness. That didn't work very well, as you can imagine. I've really been challenged to build strong friendships as I've read how God used friends in your life, Paul.

P: Thanks. I hope you'll tell others to put high priority on building strong friendships, in which they can minister to others and others minister to them. That makes for strong emotional stability, especially in hard times. I know what I'm talking about.

K: What have you done to keep yourself whole when the stress has been overwhelming, Paul?

> "I freely admit my weaknesses and have learned to accept them, yes even delight in them."

P: One strategy I've used is to do something about the situation if I can't handle it. When I was in Athens one time, I couldn't stand the stress of not knowing what had happened to the Thessalonian believers. So Silas and I sent Timothy to check on them.

Another time in Troas, the Lord opened a door for the gospel, but I didn't find Titus there. I had no peace of mind, so I left there and went to Macedonia. The point is, it's better to change the situation, or even leave, than to damage yourself emotionally.

K: That's very encouraging to hear. As a counselor, I've had to help those who stayed in situations longer than they should have and suffered severe mental and physical problems. A lot of them aren't even serving God today as a result. We sometimes call it "burnout." We seem to see it as a major failure if we can't handle every situation, but you're giving us permission to get out if we need to. I'll pass that on. Can you share anything else that helps you?

P: I've built a couple of habits over the years that no Christian should be without. First, I've learned to choose an *attitude of gratitude*, no matter how difficult things are. Long ago I learned that even when I feel terrible emotionally, I can choose to be grateful to God. It's still hard to do at times, but God always brings emotional stability when I choose to thank and praise Him.

As you know, I told the Corinthians about the time I had

no peace of mind in Troas and left. Remember what I said next? "But thanks be to God." Even when I felt I had to miss a great opportunity for the gospel, I still chose an attitude of gratitude.

A second habit I keep working on is to choose joy, especially in hard times. Did you know we have a *choice to rejoice*, no matter what the circumstances? If only Christians in your time could build this habit, I'm sure they would have a lot less emotional upheaval. What do you think?

K: I agree. In fact, I try to follow your example of choosing joy, and the Lord really does give joy, even in very difficult times. Did you know that you mentioned joy fourteen times in your letter to the Philippians? And you were in prison at the time! Paul, I want you to know that the Lord has never failed to give me joy when I've chosen gratitude and joy. I'm very grateful to you for showing me the way.

P: It's really the Lord who shows us the way. Remember, Jesus endured the cross for the joy set before Him. Hey, they're going to be changing guards soon. Any other questions?

K: This has been a great help, and I can't wait to share it with other Christians. Before I go, can you just briefly mention a few other strategies you've used to handle all that stress over the years? I hope my friends can study them in more detail and learn how to apply them.

P: Sure. I'll just run through several, but I won't tell you where they are in the Bible. Your friends should be mature enough to find them without help.

I keep working at relying on the Lord, not on myself. Of course I don't have all the modern equipment you people have, so it's easier for me to rely on the Lord than for you.

I refuse to compare myself with others. I wish every Christian would learn to do that. Comparing ourselves causes such emotional uproar.

I freely admit my weaknesses and have learned to accept

them, yes even delight in them. That brings great peace of mind and joy in the Lord.

I've had my share of conflicts with others, including Barnabas and Peter, but I didn't run away. Dealing openly with conflicts was painful for me, but it sure helps me to stay emotionally healthy.

When things look impossible, I choose to believe God. As you must know, Ken, emotional health for us depends on choosing to trust in Him, especially when doubts try to take over our minds and hearts.

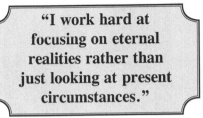

"I work hard at focusing on eternal realities rather than just looking at present circumstances."

Finally, I work hard at focusing on eternal realities rather than just looking at present circumstances. This helps me not to lose heart when times are tough.

K: Paul, I'll pass these insights on, and hope that many Christians will work on following your example, as you have followed Christ's example. As they do, I'm sure they will experience the same joy and emotional health you have, even in tough times. Thanks so much.

Questions for personal or group study

1. What stood out to you as you read the interview with Paul?

2. If you could ask Paul one question, what would it be? Why would you ask it?

3. Here are some verses about how Paul handled his stress. Read

each and discuss what you learn:

2 Corinthians 1:8-11

2 Corinthians 4:8-9, 16-18

2 Corinthians 6:4-10

1 Thessalonians 3:4-7

2 Timothy 1:16-18

Acts 16:22-25

Philippians 3:13-14

What can I do *today* to lower my stress?

1. What one or two things mentioned by Paul can you apply to your life that will reduce our stress?

2. Continue to work on the list of stressors you began in chapter four. Add more as you think of them. Ask God to reveal any sources of stress you're not aware of.

3. If you haven't done this already, write out a plan of action for each major stressor that you want to begin handling better. Consider and answer these questions:

   a. What can I do to change the situation, even a little?

   b. If I can't do anything about the situation, what can I begin doing to cope better?

   c. What internal stress is making it worse?

   d. What resources do I need to use to help me cope?

   e. What insights in these materials are of help in managing this stress better?

4. Memorize a few verses from the materials that will help you cope better with stress. Where will you begin?

5. Write at least one thing on the *Snapshots* pages (at the end of the book) that you want to remember and/or do. How can you apply it today?

How can I help others?

1. For adults, share what you learned from or about the apostle Paul from this chapter.

2. For children:

   a. Talk on their level about who Paul was and how he handled the hard times in his life. It's good for children, even at an early age, to begin to hear biblical principles on how to deal with difficulties.

   b. If there were any areas from this chapter that you think might specifically address an issue your child is having, you could focus on those. For example, if your child is a grumbler, you might talk about having an "attitude of gratitude."

---

* Note: we are not trying to say that this actually happened. However, it is a fun, different way to discover some of the principles and strategies that the Apostle Paul employed.

Part Four:
Recover Your Sanity

I (Gaylyn) felt like I was teetering on a wobbly tight rope, hopelessly trying to juggle too many balls. I don't recommend juggling while tight rope walking—never mind that I've never been good at either one. You've got to question my sanity!

But, that's what I was doing—well, I was trying anyway. When I first started a single-parent family ministry with the Navigators in 1997, I was walking a tight rope (being a single mom) and trying to juggle *way* too many balls in the ministry. Here are just a few of the things I was doing:

- Preparing and teaching weekly classes for single parents
- Ordering and distributing food from a food bank every week
- Making a meal for 40-50 people once a month
- Organizing weekly activities for the single-parent families
- Counseling single parents
- Keeping up with ministry paperwork
- Answering phone calls night and day from single parents in distress (or just wanting to chat—at midnight!)
- Creating and distributing fliers about the ministry
- Raising funds for the ministry and my little family

But that wasn't all. These were on top of my personal responsibilities as a single mom, trying to do everything that both a mother and father would do in the home. I thought I had to do it all, otherwise I wouldn't be considered spiritual or successful. Can you see any of my internal stress at work here? I had worked through a lot—but definitely not all—of my issues.

I found out that juggling too many balls didn't work. Oh, yes, for a while I was able to keep them all in the air. But when I dropped one of them, they all started to fall.

I went through a time of near burnout. I was tired of the ministry and tired of life. I just wanted to quit everything. It wasn't worth it. *I can't do this anymore. It's too much. I quit! Everyone expects me to be a superhero, to do everything. I'm only one person. Why won't anyone help me? I can't do it all.*

That was the beginning of recovering my sanity. Although, I must say, there are probably people who question whether I really am sane. So long as I feel sane, I guess I'm fine, right?

Over the coming days and weeks, I began evaluating all the things I was doing. I listed them all out and prioritized them. I spent time alone with the Lord to determine His priorities for me. I also sought counsel to help me sort through everything.

I learned that I didn't have to do everything myself. I needed to ask for help. And if I couldn't get the help, there were some "good" things I had to let go—especially in the ministry (or an expectation of always keeping the house clean!)

It took time to regain balance in my life, but it was worth it. Even still I have times when I am doing too much. (You don't think I'm an overachiever, do you?) Regularly, I need to re-evaluate all I'm doing, with the Lord's help.

Obviously, my life was not balanced, when I first started the single-parent family ministry. (That's a major understatement.) We want to challenge you to evaluate your own life as you go through this section to discover how balanced it is. You might want to figure out what you need to do to recover your sanity.

Chapter 13

Examine Your Lifestyle
How do you know if your life is balanced?

*Come to me, all you who are weary and
burdened,
and I will give you rest.
Take my yoke upon you and learn from me,
for I am gentle and humble in heart,
and you will find rest for your souls.
For my yoke is easy and my burden is light.*
Matthew 11:28-30

Over the long haul, one area that causes great pain and damage for individuals and their families is a failure to live a balanced life. Balance is as essential as food, air and water. If we try to go without balance in our lives for too long, we begin to wither and die—emotionally, spiritually and interpersonally. And so do our families and our ministries.

Another word for balance is margin. Look at the margins around this page. Imagine that the words went all the way to every

> **One area that causes great pain and damage for individuals and their families is a failure to live a balanced life.**

side of the page—that there was no white space at all. Would you like to read it? It would get you tired and overwhelmed just trying to read it. Yet, that's what we do with our lives sometimes. We use up every bit of our time, energy and money, so there is nothing left over.

Balance is having a sufficient reserve of...
Time
Energy

- *Spiritual energy*
- *Emotional energy*
- *Interpersonal energy*
- *Physical energy*

Money
... to provide for our needs
... and for the needs of others.

Consider each aspect of this definition:
1. **Sufficient reserve.** This means having what we need to handle life's unplanned and unexpected demands and opportunities. When we live with balance, we have something stored up to provide for ourselves and others when special needs arise.

   a. "Sufficient" doesn't mean we will *always* have enough

time, energy and money to meet the unexpected.

b. Sometimes unplanned events will overwhelm our reserve and leave us depleted. But if our *norm* is to have balance, we will be able to replenish our reserve in good time, without damaging ourselves and/or others.

c. A reserve is meant to be used in times of need.

d. It isn't for us to selfishly hoard.

e. Our reserve in each of these areas will normally fluctuate between "full" and "low."

f. When an area of balance begins to get low, we need to consciously plan on how to replenish it.

2. **Time.** Time is probably the *only* resource we have that is not renewable.

a. Lost or wasted time can never be recovered.

b. Time spent on *good* activities that rob us from the *best* is gone forever.

c. As precious as time is, it seems to be one of the most difficult resources to use wisely.

d. In our modern culture, maintaining a reserve of time is rarely valued.

e. We honor those who fill their schedules to the maximum.

f. To build a sufficient reserve of time requires:

- going against what many others value resolve to clearly define your priorities

- self-discipline

- a willingness to say "no" to demands that constantly confront us

> **Time spent on good activities that rob us from the best is gone forever.**

3. **Energy.** Our energy levels are very important to balance.

- We need to have a reserve of energy to meet unplanned and unexpected demands and opportunities.

- Each person has different levels of each kind of energy.

- We are unique in what charges our energy batteries and what depletes them.

a. *Spiritual energy.* We who are in "full-time" Christian service are sometimes in greater danger of depleting our spiritual energy.

- We may give so much in our ministry to others that we have little left for ourselves and for our family.

- We must know what replenishes our spiritual energy, and give high priority to maintaining it.

- Jesus is our example in this. Luke 5:15-16 says, "Yet the news about him spread all the more, so that crowds of people came to hear him and to be healed of their sicknesses. But Jesus often withdrew to lonely places and prayed."

b. *Emotional energy.* The stress and demands of our lifestyle tend to deplete us emotionally, especially if we are deeply involved in others' lives. Ministry often puts us in the same relationships Paul described in 1 Thessalonians 2:8: "We loved you so much that we were delighted to share with you not only the gospel of God but our lives (RSV: "our very selves"] as well, because you had become so dear to us." Therefore, we must give attention to engaging in whatever helps to renew our emotional energy.

c. *Interpersonal energy.*

- We don't often think of this, but we can be involved with people so much that we run out of the ability to be with them.

- Introverts drain their batteries by being with people.

Many extroverts have a difficult time understanding this, because they usually get *energized* by being with people, up to a point.

- If our interpersonal energy batteries are drained from being with others, it may be that the spiritual thing to do is to get alone and recharge ourselves.

d. *Physical energy*. This is easy for most of us to recognize, because we know what getting tired physically feels like. However, we also need to be aware of the difference between a healthy tiredness, and an unhealthy, destructive fatigue. If we work hard and get tired, but awake with new energy for the day, we have balance in our lives. But if we go through week after week and even month after month in constant

> **If our interpersonal energy batteries are drained from being with others, it may be that the spiritual thing to do is to get alone, and recharge ourselves.**

exhaustion and times of rest don't seem to help much, we are living in a dangerous state of having no balance in this area.

4. **Money.** God may want us to live at times with no balance in finances. We can learn trust and dependence on Him in such times. And yet, it may be that He desires that we would *normally* live with a money balance. If we believe this is true for us, we need to faithfully ask Him to provide it in His way and His time. Just as with our time and energy, the purpose of having balance in our money is not only to meet our unplanned needs; with money balance we can also help with the financial needs of others.

5. **To provide for our needs and for the needs of others.** Obviously, one purpose of having balance is so that we can

meet our own needs in the unexpected demands of life. In fact, if we can't meet our own needs, we have nothing to give to others. But having balance for the needs of others is just as important. "Others" includes our immediate family, extended family, friends, co-workers, and any others God has brought into our lives in significant ways.

How Well Am I Living A Balanced Life?

Consider how you are at maintaining balance, and use this scale to indicate your responses. In the left column describe yourself. In the right column describe how you think your spouse, your children or a close friend might perceive you. Be honest as you go through this.

*1 = Hardly ever, 2 = Occasionally, 3 = Sometimes,
4 = Often, 5 = Nearly always*

Self   Other

____ ____ 1.   I am able to keep up with my workload without robbing time from other important things and people in my life.

____ ____ 2.   My lifestyle is characterized by love, joy, peace and patience.

____ ____ 3.   When there is more work than I can handle, I can leave it, physically and mentally, so that it doesn't bother me after work.

____ ____ 4.   I have ample time and energy to enjoy my friends.

____ ____ 5.   I take a day of rest weekly.

____ ____ 6. I get enough sleep to maintain good physical and mental well-being.

____ ____ 7. When those close to me need to spend time with me, I have the time.

____ ____ 8. I am able to help others financially when they are in need.

____ ____ 9. I take all the time I need to spend with the Lord, without feeling hurried or hassled.

____ ____ 10. I am able to maintain sufficient communication with friends, family and others who are important to me.

____ ____ 11. I know what "charges my spiritual, emotional and physical batteries" and I consistently take time to do so.

For Married People:

____ ____ 12. My spouse is happy with the amount of time and energy I have for him or her.

____ ____ 13. I am happy with the amount and quality of time I am able to spend with my spouse.

For Parents:

____ ____ 14. My children are happy with the amount of time and energy I have for them.

____ ____ 15. I give adequate time for planned and/or regular family activities.

____ ____ 16. When I'm with my family, I'm free from concerns about other responsibilities and problems.

1. Pick one or two of your lowest scores to begin working on.

2. How did you score yourself, compared to how someone else would score you?

3. If you are not sure that you have an accurate view of yourself, ask someone close to you to rate you on this assessment. You might be surprised what you learn. Even if you think you have an accurate view, it might be very enlightening to see how someone else views you and how you deal with stress.

Key Issues About Living a Balanced Life

Here are three issues to consider regarding living a balanced life. You may want to revise them to reflect more accurately what you believe and how you live.

These are some core beliefs that you may or may not hold. Read them and figure out what you believe about each topic.

Issue #1
Living a balanced life is *my* responsibility. I cannot give it away to God, my supervisor, or anyone else.

1. Do you really believe this? Or do you think that it's up to others to keep your life balanced? Explain.

2. How could you reword it to reflect more accurately how you actually live?

3. If you are struggling to believe this, consider this question: "If I really believed and lived this, how might it affect my life?"

4. Have you turned the responsibility for your life over to others? If so, to whom? And, how can you take that responsibility back?

Issue #2
If I don't control my schedule and pressures, Satan may do it for me.

1. Really consider this issue. Do you believe it?

2. Look back on your life. When has this been true for you?

3. If you haven't been in control of your schedule, what might you need to do to take the control back?

Issue #3
If I have more than I can possibly do, it is probably not all from God.

1. Look back on your life. When has this been true for you? What about right now?

2. If you have too much to do, take some time to ask the Lord what His priorities are for you.

3. Review the definition of "Junk Stress" in Chapter 3. You can modify it for maintaining balance by rewording it to say, "Any activity/commitment/responsibility/duty in which the cost of keeping it is greater than the benefits and it is not sin to dump it." Try to identify at least one thing you're doing that fits this definition, and consider how to stop doing it.

What can I do *today* to bring more balance Into my life?

1. What do you need to change to have a more balanced life?

2. Write out a commitment describing specifically what you will do to have more balance in your life.

3. Choose one of the verses in this chapter to write on a card to remind you to stay balanced.

4. Write at least one thing on the *Snapshots* pages (at the end of the book) that you want to remember and/or do. How can you apply it today?

Questions for personal or group study

1. Think about or discuss each part of the definition of balance, at the beginning of this chapter. What stands out to you?

2. Where do you struggle the most to maintain balance in your life?

3. What can others help you do to maintain balance in your life? Who will you ask? When will you ask him/her?

4. Consider Jesus' teaching and example in the following verses. What can you learn from Him about maintaining balance? Look up as many of the verses as you can.

   a. Physical Balance:

      Mark 6:31-32

      Luke 8:22-23

b. Spiritual Balance

Luke 5:15-16

Mark 1:35

c. Emotional Balance

Matthew 11:28-30

d. Financial Balance

Proverbs 27:23-27

Luke 6:38

2 Corinthians 9:6-12

e. Balance for the Needs of Others

Matthew 20:29-34

Mark 10:13-16 (The disciples were upset because they thought Jesus was too *busy* to be bothered by children.)

How can I help others?

1. For adults:

   a. Share any areas where you struggle to maintain balance. That can open the door for them to share their struggles.

   b. Ask if there is anything you can do to help them achieve a greater stability in their lives.

   c. Ask yourself, *Am I in any way causing those close to me to struggle with their balance? What expectations, demands or requests am I needlessly putting on them?*

2. For children:

   a. Consider your responses to the self assessment in the section on children. Which areas need work?

   b. Is there anything you are doing that might be modeling a lack of balance for your children? Remember they will follow your example. What might you need to change?

Chapter 14

Design Your Strategy
How do you successfully juggle life's demands?

Very few, *if any,* people achieve and maintain balance without a deliberate strategy to do so. It just doesn't happen automatically. Everything around us pressures us to live to the very limit of our capacity, leaving us nothing in reserve.

Go back and reread the section on saying a "prayerful no" on page 39. This same skill can be one of your best ways to maintain balance. In fact, we believe it is an essential part of maintaining balance.

A serious problem with lack of balance is that we don't have time to work on it! If you are struggling in this area, you will have a strong compulsion to go back to your "normal" life, and fail to take the time and effort needed to change.

Many of us grow more effectively if we don't feel overwhelmed by trying to work on too many issues at once.

Leave Work at Work

To maintain balance, most people must make clear time and space barriers between work and the rest of their lives. This is especially true if you run your own business. If you have difficulty with this, try the following steps:

1. **Working in the home.** There are times when working in your home is your best option. For example, when my (Gaylyn's) children were young, I enjoyed working at home, because I could be available to them whenever they needed me. It is definitely a balancing act to try to work at home, and it will test your sanity. If your office is in your home, consider these issues:

   a. If you work in your home, what are your reasons?

   b. What effects does this have on you and those with whom you live? Ask those who live in your home how it affects them.

   c. Note what options you have for changing this, and list positive and negative effects of any options which may be viable.

   d. If you choose an option, write what you will do and when.

> ## A serious problem with lack of balance is that we don't have time to work on it!

2. **Bringing work home.**

   a. Do you bring your work home? If so, what are your reasons? How often?

   b. Are you satisfied that this is right for you and your family, if you have one?

   c. Note any positive and negative consequences of doing it.

   d. Ask your family or a close friend how they see it.

   e. Based on your responses and theirs, decide what you want to do. Will you continue as you're doing now, set limits on how much and how often, or stop altogether?

   f. Write out your decisions. Try them for a month and then reevaluate.

3. **Mentally taking work home.** Do you take your work home mentally and emotionally at times, or are you able to go home and be free from thinking about it and/or feeling anxious over it? Ask those close to you what they think.

   If you have difficulty in this area, try the following ideas:

a. Describe what you think about or feel anxious about, such as: too much work, work not done well, work too difficult, interpersonal conflicts, time pressures, deadlines, interruptions, difficult decisions, others' problems, etc.

b. Then try this technique for two weeks: before leaving work each day, get alone with the Lord. Tell Him verbally or in writing what is bothering you. Give it to Him to hold until you return to work again (Psa. 55:22; 1 Pet. 5:7).

It may help to visualize stuffing your work problems into a garbage bag, tying it tight so the fumes can't get out, and dumping it into His hands. If you take it back (and you probably will), just give it back again, and keep doing it until you can let go. This process takes practice, so keep at it until you learn to do it consistently.

c. If you're in the habit of discussing work problems at home, especially at the dinner table, ask yourself and your family if this helps create a happy environment for everyone, and if it fits the criteria in Philippians 4:8. If not, agree together that you will no longer discuss work problems, especially during meals. You might set aside some time to discuss issues at another time.

Handle Your Guilt

Guilt over work or other things left undone, or not done as well as it might have been, is a significant problem for many people. Another problem is guilt over not living up to other people's expectations of them.

1. **If you experience guilt in any area, try to identify specifically what you feel guilty about.**

2. **Try to determine if this is true or false guilt.** True guilt is when God judges us as guilty, because we have actually done something wrong. False guilt is feeling guilty when we judge ourselves as guilty, but God does not.

    You can feel guilty and not be guilty. If in doubt as to whether it's true or false, look in God's Word. If you are still in doubt, ask someone you trust what they think. If you decide it is true guilt, confess it and decide what you can do to change your behavior. If it is false guilt, acknowledge it to yourself and God, thank Him that He is not condemning you (Rom. 8:1), and claim His promises that you aren't condemned.

Handle Pressures

We must be skilled in managing pressures, requests and demands in a godly and wise way if we are to maintain balance. Here is a helpful process for doing this that you may want to try.

1. **Clarify your values.**

    a. To get a better perspective on these life values, list each person, relationship, activity, object, etc. you consider important. (If you need more space, use a separate sheet)

    b. Then place a value of **1, 2** or **3** before each one, with **1** being of highest value. Examples might include your relationship to Christ, your spouse, children or team members, health, work, ministry to others, intellectual growth, emotional well-being, etc.

    c. Keep these values in mind as you work through the rest of the strategy.

2. **Prioritize your tasks.**

    a. List each activity outside of work, sleep and meals that requires more than one hour per week.

    b. Note how much time you average weekly on each task.

    c. Then place a priority on each responsibility:

    > **1 = absolutely necessary**
    > **2 = very important but not absolutely necessary**
    > **3 = good but could be dropped without serious consequences**

3. **Consider and apply options.** Consider these questions:

a. Of priority **1** and **2** responsibilities, can any be delegated? If so, to whom?

b. Among priority **3** responsibilities, which ones are you willing to drop completely? Weigh possible positive and negative consequences of dropping each one. Decide which ones can be dropped and drop them.

c. Of the remaining priority 3 responsibilities:

- Decide which can be put into a group which would only be done if all priority **1** and **2** responsibilities were under control. (Possibly all priority **3** responsibilities will fit in this group.)

- Then decide that you will not do these responsibilities unless all others are handled. This group then becomes a "guilt-free" area of your life.

- You (and your supervisor, if these priorities relate to your work) should agree that there will be no blame or guilt over not doing these responsibilities.

- They can be reconsidered at any time, to be dropped, delegated or moved up in priority.

  If you still have more responsibilities than can be handled, look over the rest of them, and ask if any of them can be delegated, or relegated to a lower priority. If any can be delegated, decide to whom, when, and who will do the delegating.

d. Look at the remaining responsibilities, and consider these questions:

- In what ways can I do this more efficiently?

- Must it be done as completely or as perfectly as I am now doing it? Not everything worth doing is worth doing well!

- Who might I ask to help me with it?

- What other resources am I utilizing or have I not yet used?

- Who is equipped to give me ideas on how to do it in less time and/or better?

4. Write out any conclusions and decisions you make. Try them and note the results.

Not everything worth doing is worth doing well!

Questions for personal or group study

1. In what areas do you struggle most to keep a balanced life?

2. What is one thing that could help you keep more balanced?

3. Look up each verse in this chapter and consider what you can learn from it.

4. What do you need to do to bring a greater balance into your life?

5. What can you let go of or delegate to someone else?

6. Look at Jesus' example in Luke 5:15-16. What do you learn from it?

What can I do *today* to recover my balance?

1. List all the things you are doing right now, both in your personal life and at work. You might need a separate sheet.

2. Pick at least one thing from your list that you will let go or delegate to someone else. Write it down.

3. Look over the strategies you wrote down, earlier in this chapter.

   a. Choose just two or three to focus on first. If you try to work on too many things at once, you will get overwhelmed and discouraged and you will probably not do any of them.

   b. When those are working for you, go back and choose one or two more.

4. Find someone who you can talk to, who will hold you accountable to become more balanced.

Remember: new habits generally take a few months to become part of us, so don't be in too much of a hurry.

How can I help others?

1. **For adults and teens:** If you know someone who struggles with being overwhelmed by too much to do, ask if he would like to talk about what might help. If he says "yes," walk through the steps in "Optimize Your Success."

2. Children often suffer when their parents have a lack of balance in their lives.

   a. Consider how your choices may affect your children. Talk about this with your spouse or a close friend. Sometimes we can't see the results of our choices, because we are too close to the issues. Write down what you discover and any changes you need to make.

   b. Ask them what they would like you to do differently.

   c. If your choices are hurting your children, take the time to work through each section in this chapter. Then make your children a priority. They are God's gift to you.

Congratulations. You finished the book. You now have the tools you need to handle any stress situations that arise. We want to encourage you to continue to apply the skills to your life. The more you practice, the easier they will become. If you didn't have time to look up each Bible verse, you might want to do that in your daily Bible Study. You also have your "Snapshots" sheets as a reminder of your chapter highlights.

We pray God's abundant blessings on you as you continue to follow Him.

Ken & Gaylyn

Appendix A
Small Groups

You will learn so much more if you study this book in a small group or at least with one other person. The purposes of small groups are to:

1. Talk about issues of growth
2. Minister to each other
3. Be ministered to
4. Study with others what God's Word says about each topic
5. Hold each other accountable

It will help if you choose a group leader who can keep the discussion going. If you would like more help on this, please contact Relationship Resources for materials on leading groups effectively.

At your first meeting, ask everyone to make a verbal commitment to keep everything heard in the group confidential—even if you don't think the person would mind if you shared it with others. Commit to only sharing anything you hear in the group *if* you have specific permission to share it.

Group Discussions

Give everyone the opportunity to share in discussions—only if they want to. Some people are naturally more talkative and are eager to make a contribution often. And some are more reticent to share. It takes some people longer than others to formulate their ideas. Silence during group discussions can be an effective way to draw these people out. Others feel uncomfortable during silence and want to fill it with talk. In the first meeting, agree that you will accept silence as good.

We encourage those of you who find it easy to speak up in groups to be aware of those who don't find it easy. Be "slow to speak and quick to listen." If you have already spoken to the issue at hand, be slow to share more until others have had ample opportunity to talk.

Do not ever call on anyone to answer a question, unless they have indicated that they want to share on that question. Calling on people who do not want to share on a given topic, can make the atmosphere in the group unsafe for them and for others. This is especially true for people who are introverts—like we both are. Extroverts (who usually lead groups) may not understand this concept, because they are usually comfortable sharing in a group.

Relationship Resources has more information on how to lead groups effectively, people want to come back and so their lives are changed. For more help on leading a group using this book, contact us at groups@RelationshipResources.org.

Leader's Guide

You can study this book with a group in a variety of ways. Depending on how many sessions you want to meet, each week could study:

One "Part" of the book

One chapter

More than one chapter. The following chapters are easily combined for one session:

- 1-3
- 4-6
- 7-9
- 10-13
- 14-15
- 16-17

Use the questions at the end of each chapter for group discussions. If you are combining more than one chapter, you can choose which of the questions to discuss.

Appendix B
About Us

Relationship Resources...
- Facilitates growth for believers and not-yet-believers in their relationships with God, themselves and other people
- Provides practical, biblical, interactive workshops and materials designed to empower and equip individuals and groups in their lives, work and ministries
- Trains and mentors facilitators to provide their workshops for other groups
- Gained IRS nonprofit status in 1999
- Began as a concept in 1970 with Ken Williams training missionaries

Gaylyn Williams is...
- The director of Relationship Resources, Inc., since 1999
- Passionate about empowering people for maximum success in their lives and relationships

- A published author with sixteen books
- A magazine writer with numerous published articles in various magazines.
- An international motivational speaker and seminar trainer
- Mother of two grown sons
- A former missionary with Wycliffe Bible Translators from 1972 to 1992
- A former missionary with The Navigators from 1997-1999

Gaylyn can be contacted at gaylyn@rrbooks.org.

For more information, go to www.RelationshipResources.org.

International Training Partners (ITP):

- founded by Dr. Ken Williams who is now Vice President.

- a global network of trainers from more than eighty organizations. They serve together in an informal partnership to provide practical, interactive, biblical training in interpersonal relationships for Christian workers.

- more than 500 trainers have been equipped from many nationalities, representing more than eighty organizations.

- approximately 800 workshops have been held in service to more than 16,000 Christian workers in at least eighty-one countries.

- The training materials have been translated into several languages.

Dr. Ken Williams:

He and his wife Bobbie began their ministry with Wycliffe Bible Translators in 1957. They first served among the Chuj people of Guatemala, completing a translation of the New Testament, as well as founding a Bible Institute, literacy work, and medical clinics. In the early 1970's Ken began providing care and counseling for cross-cultural workers. Ken earned his Ph.D. in Human Behavior, and he and Bobbie continued in this ministry with WBT for 22 years, counseling thousands of missionaries worldwide.

Ken came to realize that many of the difficult issues addressed in counseling could be avoided if believers received effective training in interpersonal relationships and managing stress. This was accompanied by Ken's deep conviction that healthy, godly relationships are best built and sustained by living out God's word.

In 1987 Ken began to develop training programs for workers in Christian ministries, especially mission organizations. Ken may be contacted at ken@rrbooks.org.

For more information, go to www.itpartners.org.

Workshop and Seminar Endorsements

These are just a few of the comments we have received from people who have attended our workshops:

Is it really possible to live in joy when your life has been riddled with unthinkable pain? I am awed by a person who has mastered the task. Gaylyn shares a litany of life events that would have sent Goliath spiraling. Much like David the shepherd boy, she faced off with her giant and moved from defeat to victory! Her story held me captive—the unabridged truth came with force and clarity. It was clear she had spent time in the soul's abyss and came out a shining star. She is amazingly authentic.

—*Kimberly Faye*, Author and Speaker

Gaylyn Williams and her incredible life story and spirit inspire all those who are fortunate enough to hear her speak or read her story. Gaylyn's humble, but powerful, style is laced with humor, grace, heartache, and joy, while her story embodies adventure, courage, triumph, and tragedy. By creatively sharing the lessons she learned along the way, Gaylyn helps the rest of us see how we too can apply those lessons to ease our own burdens.

—*Kris Harty*, Author, Speaker and Stickabilities Specialist
www.StrongSpiritUnlimited.com

This is the only seminar/workshop I have ever come home from feeling like I could do what they taught because I had done it.

—*Beverly, Texas*

A simple increase in knowledge about relationships isn't enough to change behavior. Practice is the key and practice is at the core of this workshop. This material applies to every area of my life.

—*Human Resources Director, Florida*

Every time I have the opportunity to study this material with you, I'm blown away. I truly come home refreshed and inspired. The material is so much more believable, because I can see how you are applying it in your lives.

—Lee Ann, Texas

I'm going to be different, not overnight but over the long haul. Here was a workshop that was not hype, emotions and fluff, but nuts and bolts, hammer and trowel foundational stuff! It needs to be a slow-drip learning for lifelong change.

—John, Texas

I came here thinking this was just going to help me 'on the job' but throughout the week it became more and more obvious that all of this applies to how I interact as a wife and mom! If you don't practice this at home, don't try to export it outside your home to your business! It was like attending a marriage building seminar without my spouse!

—Nancy, Kenya

This was the best course we have ever had at our university. It is a lot of fun and the students are really participating.

—Professor, Amman, Jordan

This was the best workshop I've ever attended. It transformed parts of my own personal life. It was extremely helpful for my work. The written material is marvelous.

—A leader in Kenya

The workshop surpassed all our expectations in the deep learning, vulnerability, and obvious change that took place before our very eyes on a daily basis. Participants and non-participants are talking about the visible positive results in meetings and personal interactions that they observed to be directly attributed to the workshop."

Ed, Ecuador

More Endorsements for This Book

Solidly based on God's Word, this book will help the reader maintain a healthy perspective even facing cross-cultural stressors. With the focus on practical tools, there are exercises to think through personal application of the information as well as to utilize with a group or pass along to other people helpers as well.
—*Kenneth Royer*, Director of Missionary Care,
Link Care Center

We've never read a book like it. It's not a one-time-sitting read. It is meant to be read slowly and carefully, and there is work to do when reading it....heart work. The book has shown us our needs and pointed us faithfully to Scripture for the answers.
—*Jim & Gail McKelvey*, Missionaries with CAM International

During the time that I was an engineer in aerospace for 33 years, I was frequently faced with pressures and managerial duties. If this wonderful book had been available to me during this period of my life, I could have handled the many pressures in this line of work with a better knowledge and foresight using the tools available. I would highly recommend this book to everyone.
—*Kym Kymla*, Retired Engineer

This refreshingly simple book is filled with usable, practical advice in dealing with the stressors of life. It is rich in biblical content and will lead the reader to a place of hope and balance. This is a tool that I will personally use! I have used many of these principles over the years and found them to be profitable when applied on a consistent basis.
—George Stahnke, Director of Renewal Ministries

Readers will benefit greatly from these stories, experiences and the practical, biblical principles.
—*Joe Sabah*, author of *How to Get on Radio Talk Shows All Across America*

When Dr. Ken Williams shared this material, a light came on. For the first time many of our workers had some effective tools to help them deal with the very considerable stresses that cross-cultural service inevitably involves. I am thrilled that Ken and Gaylyn have teamed up to make this material available in book form. I commend the book to all who are involved in Christian service, however, every believer would benefit from this material.
—*Frank Hoskin*, Director, Wycliffe Bible Translators Australia

This book is the best material I have found on handling stress. The principles are solidly Biblical, born out of real life experience facing stress. I will encourage all of our missionaries in TEAM to get and work through it. I am grateful for this new resource that they can use. Thank you again for this book and the potential it has to help missionaries and many others with their stress.
—*Steven G. Edlin* MA LCPC MFT, Counseling Director,
TEAM

There is hope for us stressed out 21st century folks! The book is also not a wishy washy, preachy, pat answer kind of book…the reader who chooses, gets deep into the principles, God's Word and examines his or her own way of coping. It is about, and for, REAL people dealing with REAL stress.
—*Jane Neiswender*, Dir. of Counseling Ministries, WBT USA

All Stressed Up and Everywhere to Go not only brings understanding to the issues of what stress is, but it also gives practical and concrete strategies for attaining spiritual, emotional, physical and interpersonal balance. Now who, in this day and age, wouldn't want that?!
—*Leta Van Meter*, Trainer with Paraklete Mission Group

This is an incredible book especially for today's world. Gaylyn and Ken teach practical techniques that anyone can use to learn how to manage stress, to relax, and to enjoy life again.
—*Dwan Bent Twyford*, Author of *How to Sell A House When It is Worth Less Than You Owe*

Appendix C
More Biblical Resources

You may want to spend some time in God's Word and dig out for yourself some of the many rich nuggets of truth about stress. One fruitful way of doing so is to look in depth at the lives of Jesus, Paul, David and other biblical characters. The following areas of study may be helpful. Scriptural examples are noted to give you ideas.

Kinds of stress situations they encountered (2 Cor. 4:8-12).

Distresses they experienced under stress (Luke 22:44).

Symptoms of stress they experienced (Luke 22:44).

Commands on how to deal with stress (Matt. 6:25).

Their responses to God under stress (Acts 16:22-25).

Other strategies for coping (2 Cor. 1:10-11).

God's character as a resource (2 Thess. 3:3).

God's intervention (2 Tim. 4:16-18).

God's purposes in stress and suffering (2 Cor. 1:9).

Spiritual resources to use for stress (Rom. 15:4).

Results of managing stress well (1 Pet. 5:10).

Key Elements in Hebrews on Renewing Our Minds

The book of Hebrews is a helpful handbook for handling stress.

- It gives us a glimpse of the mighty, eternal Son of God, Creator of the universe, with abundant power to renew us.

- It also reveals the humble Savior, who became like us so that he could truly empathize with our weaknesses.

Both of these facets of Christ are needed for renewing our minds.

Hebrews gives us at least six key elements for renewing our minds. These are described throughout the Word.

As you go through this section, look up each verse and mark which specific aspects you want to work on.

1. **The Word of God.** Hebrews 4:12-13. God's Word has power to pierce our soul, mind and spirit. As it penetrates our innermost being, it brings:

   - revival

   - wisdom

   - joy

   - enlightenment

   According to Hebrews 2:1, we must pay careful attention to the Word. *Meditating* on God's Word renews our minds. As it penetrates deeply, it corrects wrong attitudes and challenges unrealistic expectations. See Psalm 1:2, 19:7-8; 107:20.

2. **Prayer.** Hebrews 4:14-16. Prayer brings gracious help from our sympathetic High Priest to deal with weaknesses, including

attitudes and expectations which need renewing. Because He experienced the reality of our humanness, we can trust Him for mercy and grace to help us in our times of need.

3. **Faith.** Hebrews 11:23-26. Moses is only one example of a person whose mind was renewed through faith. Our trust in God empowers and motivates us to line up our thoughts and attitudes to be like His.

4. **Focus on Jesus.** Hebrews 12:2-3. Let us fix our eyes on Jesus, and consider Him, so we won't grow weary and lose heart. It's revealing to take a good look at ourselves in the light of the Word. But then we must turn our minds from ourselves to Jesus. As we do, we experience His renewing.

5. **Ministry of Others.** Hebrews 3:13; 10:24-25. Other people in the body of Christ are powerful instruments in God's hands for renewing our minds. We need others to help clarify our expectations, and to confront our destructive attitudes.

6. **Action.** Hebrews 12:1-3. Our actions are based on:

   - the Word
   - prayer
   - faith

   We are to actively lay aside everything that hinders us, including our sins, and to run our race with perseverance. The Bible gives us many other actions which help renew our minds.

As we apply these and other biblical principles in the renewing process, we experience greater and greater renewal. In the process we find that our internal stress diminishes, and we experience a healthier perception of new stress situations.

Appendix D
Getting to Know God

If you don't yet have a personal relationship with God, we encourage you to get to know Him. Here are some ways you can do that:

- Read the Bible. A good place to start is in the book of John.

- Ask Him to show Himself real to you. He will, if you really mean it.

- Learn about Him through His names. www.DailyNameofGod. com has a different name of the Lord to think about each day.

- Find a good, Bible-believing church.

- Email us to start a discussion. We'll never push you.

Romans 3:23 explains that we "all have sinned and fallen short of the glory of God." We can't have a relationship with God on our own.

Romans 6:23 tells us that as a result of sin in our lives there is price to be paid—death. But *instead* of death, God wants to give us a gift—"eternal life in Christ Jesus our Lord."

John 3:16 sheds light on how much God loves us, how desperately he wants to give us this gift of living with Him forever. We see the sacrifice he made so he *could* give us this gift. "For God so loved the world that he gave his one and only Son, that whoever believes in him shall not perish but have eternal life."

Romans 10:9 explains there are two simple things you and I need to do in order to receive this gift: "If you confess with your mouth, 'Jesus is Lord,' and believe in your heart that God raised him from the dead, you will be saved."

Do these truths resonate with you? If you haven't yet trusted Jesus as your savior, you can do so right now, by praying a prayer like the following:

Dear Lord, I realize I'm a sinner and need You. Thank you for dying on the cross for my sins and rising again the third day from the dead. I now confess all my sins and repent. I ask you to forgive me and cleanse me from all sin. Thank you for saving me and making me right with you. In Jesus' name. Amen.

Look what happens in heaven the moment we put our trust in Jesus. Luke 15:7 says, "I tell you that in the same way there will be more rejoicing in heaven over one sinner who repents than over ninety-nine righteous persons who do not need to repent."

How do you respond to that?

There's no pressure to trust God immediately. He's not in a hurry, although He is waiting to talk with you. Neither of us can imagine trying to deal with our stress, without having a relationship with God and using the resources He provides.

If you just trusted Jesus as your Savior, congratulations. Now we'd encourage you to do three things:

1. Get a modern Bible at a Christian Bookstore (if you don't already have one) so you can read God's love-letters to you in familiar, contemporary language. As you read, you'll gain wonderful insights into who God is and the wonderful plans he has for you. A good place to start reading is in the book of *John.*

2. Find a Bible-believing church where you can learn and grow.

3. Email us. We'd love to know if you just trusted Jesus as your savior, so we can pray for you!

Even if you're not sure about the whole concept, we'd love to hear from you. Email us at RR@RelationshipResources.org.

Snapshots

*Write notes in each sections about what
God is saying to you for that chapter.
What do you want to remember and do?
This can become your "to do" list.*

Chapter 1
Embrace the Truth
What is stress?

Chapter 2
Recognize the Problem
Are you stressing yourself?

Chapter 3
Prevent Burnout
Are you at risk?

Chapter 4
Determine Your Stressors
What is causing your stress?

Chapter 5
Understand Your Reactions
How is stress affecting you?

Chapter 6
Stop the Pain
How do you handle your emotions?

Chapter 7
Harness Your Resources
How can you enlist God's help?

Chapter 8
Relieve the Pressure
How can you lower your stress?

Chapter 9
Transform Your Circumstances
How will focusing on God help you?

Chapter 10
Empower Your Potential
How can the Bible help you?

Chapter 11
Uncover Treasure
What other resources are available?

Chapter 12
Discover Some Amazing Secrets
What are some additional strategies?

Chapter 13
Examine Your Lifestyle
How do you know if your life is balanced?

Chapter 14
Design Your Strategy
How do you successfully juggle life's demands?